To Stephen

thank you so much for
all your encouragement

love

Dave

Reviews for *Creating a Culture of Overflow*

"I appreciate authors that take the time and energy to create a conversation around a certain topic or theme. In this book *Creating a Culture of Overflow* you will be invited into a conversation around leadership and culture. If you're a leader or person that desires to create a culture where people can thrive, this book will help you to move forward in this area. Enjoy!" **Eric Johnson, Senior Pastor at Bethel Church, Redding, California, and author of** *Christ in You*

David Elverson brings a refreshingly different perspective to leadership and disciple making. His career in the marketplace and his leadership within the church have come together for strategic insight into how we can better equip and release world changer's that carry the culture of the Kingdom. A must read for church, marketplace, and ministry leaders! **Jamie Dickson - Pastor of Kingdom Life Church Maine, NE USA Regional Director for the Burn 24/7**

"In reading this book, I came to realise that David Elverson is modelling prophecy in business. It is prophetic because I believe it is demonstrating a new kind of Christian writing about business. It breaks down the old silos of thinking and behaving. The traditional strict separation of the spiritual from business needs to be seen for what it is: a strategy of the enemy that has done untold harm. We don't need to bring "God" into business; He is already there, and is more passionate about it as an expression of His Kingdom than we are. Further, the book itself is wonderful sense-making synthesis of discipleship and practical leadership. I found it a gold mine of mature thinking, with much I can use personally in better leading a business Christ's way."

Patrick Mayfield, CEO of PearceMayfield, and author of *Practical People Engagement: Leading Change through the Power of Relationships.*

I've known Dave as a youth, a student, a husband, a businessman, a father, a leader and ultimately in all of that, as a follower of Jesus.

Creating a Culture of Overflow is a very practical book and I find it refreshing in its reflection of scripture. Having worked in business, and with people this book is written in such a way that it is a *can-do* book.

It embraces whatever style of leader you are and within it you will find something to make you a better, bigger person - it's all about reaching the potential within us and finding the flourishing in the circumstances within which we find ourselves.
Roy Crowne, Executive Director HOPE

'David Elverson has combined his skill as a Management Consultant with his knowledge of the Bible to ask the question; *"Are Churches producing members who are consumers or producers?" Are they recognising, encouraging and using the Ephesian ministries to mobilise and equip members to be fruitful and multiply? Or are they ignoring God given ministries that have been "spurned at every turn?"*

As Archbishop Justin Welby has said, all Christians need to be like champagne, bubbling over daily with 'joy and delight' as witnesses of the love of Jesus. This book encourages Church Leaders to unite, pool resources and march as one army to defeat the Satanic strongholds destroying this once great nation. **John Wright International Director, The Full Gospel Business Men's Fellowship International**

Congratulations to David for creating a wide-ranging exploration of what fullness is and how leaders can create cultures that can move themselves, their families, businesses, churches and wider communities through engagement to fullness and revival. Jesus is at the centre and is the inspiration of this book which provides practical ideas and tools based on David's personal life and experience as well as extensive research and insight. The book is a valuable resource which gives us tools to evaluate where we are and steps we can take to make ourselves and those we lead and influence, thrive. **Keith Williams former Senior Vice President of AT Kearney and Senior Consultant at Coopers & Lybrand**

As Christians, we are called to engage with and transform the cultures of this world with the cultures of the Kingdom of God – bringing heaven to earth. David draws on his particular experience as a management consultant but this book is rooted in his experience of everyday life. Well-researched, with some helpful practical exercises, it is designed to help you become a culture-changer in your own context: whether that is family, workplace or church.

Revd Stephen Mawditt. Leader of Fountain of Life church and Fountain Network

Creating a Culture of Overflow

Creating a Culture of Overflow

David Elverson
with
Paul Manwaring

Creating a Culture of Overflow
David Elverson with Paul Manwaring

Unless otherwise indicated , Scripture quotations are taken from the HOLY BIBLE, NEW INTERNATIONAL VERSION. Copyright 1973, 1978, 1984 Biblica

Scripture quotations identified AMP are from the Amplified Bible, copyright 1954, 1958, 1962, 1964, 1965, 1987 by The Lockman Foundation

The chapter included written by Paul Manwaring is an extract from Paul's series entitled Master Kingdom Administration and is used with permission.

Published in the United Kingdom by Wild Horses Publishing

ISBN 978-0-9932363-2-7

Dedication and Acknowledgements

I'd like to dedicate this book to the Holly, Olivia and Beatrice and the adventure we are on together as we follow God's leading and prompting to move from the ordinary to the world changers he has called all of us to be.

Many people have given of their time and expertise so generously to help with the writing and publishing of this book. I'd particularly like to thank Peter Adams, Patrick Mayfield, Stephen Mawditt and Ron Elverson for the invaluable wisdom they in putted into the early manuscript. I'd also like to thank Tim Elverson for his assistance in preparing the ebook version.

I'd also like to thank my wife Holly Elverson for tirelessly hearing about the latest chapter I've written, for reading them and giving her insights and for being a source of inspiration for much of what is written.

Finally I'd like to thank Paul Manwaring. Paul has not only written a chapter for this book, but is also at the centre of fathering a movement that sees the Kingdom of Heaven invade all areas of life; the workplace as well as the church! He helps the church understand what culture is and why it is important for seeing revival come and be sustained. Through the leadership development programme Paul runs (www.globallegacy.com), Holly and I have been changed as we discovered so much more of God's plans for us and for all who were created in his image!

The chapter written by Paul is an extract from his series entitled Mastering Kingdom Administration.

Contents

Preface

From time to time certain words or ways of thinking gain real traction and become 'buzz words' that are used all over the place; sometimes in context, sometimes out of context. One such word that this has happened to in recent times is 'culture'.

It has happened for very good reasons; churches and businesses have found that culture is far more important than strategy, ability or perhaps even anointing in seeing things come to fruition in a sustainable way. Culture creates an environment in which things grow, both the bad and the good. So understanding the cultures we need and the specifics of how to create these cultures is very important.

Many leaders in church and business realise 'culture' is important, but perhaps due to the intangible nature of 'culture', don't fully know why or what to do about it.

This book is designed to be a tool to help leaders get to grips with culture in a practical way. The first chapter, by Paul Manwaring looks at what culture is and why it is so important before the rest of the book further breaks down some of the constituent parts of culture and gives practical ideas for leading yourself and others to new cultures that bring life.

This book specifically explores creating a culture that frees people to live life in all of its fullness. However there maybe other elements of Kingdom culture that you want to develop and embed in your church or business. Our hope is the principles described in this book help you to implement the cultural change that is needed. Our hope is to turn an intangible word into something practical and action based that will help us all lead our churches, business and families into a revival that will overflow into a cultural reformation of society.

I hope you enjoy it

David Elverson

1

The Power of Culture

Paul Manwaring

Words and their meanings have often fascinated me, none more than the word "culture." On one level, culture is not a new concept as we have studied culture of nations and people groups since time began. Yet during the past forty to fifty years the organizational world has experienced a steady increase in the use and understanding of culture.

The introduction of culture to the corporate world has been far-reaching. Culture may very well be one of the most powerful resources available to the administrator. Management consultant Peter Drucker originated the phrase, "Culture eats strategy for breakfast." If planning and strategizing can be consumed by culture then it is no wonder there is an increasing awareness of its power and relevance.

And so it makes sense to understand what culture is, how it evolves, and the power it contains for both good and harm. While culture is not necessarily a biblical word, the concept and power of it certainly is biblical. Romans 12:2 encourages the reader to not conform to the world (culture), but rather be transformed. And of course, once we are transformed, we will transform the world around us. I have always loved the translation of this verse offered by J.B. Phillips in his version of the New Testament in Modern English, "Don't let the world around you squeeze you into its own mould…" That is a great way of describing culture: it moulds thinking, behavior, and almost all aspects of life.

There is a simple progression of a culture which is demonstrated every year in the USA. When the first Europeans arrived in the new land of America, they carried with them a history of harvest festivals. Around October each year they would have attended a church service dedicated to giving thanks for another year's harvest. Arriving in America, they again celebrated the provision of the land. That celebration was so important to them that it became an annual holiday, which then became enshrined in law. Over 200 years later, Americans stop work on the fourth Thursday of November and, as many as possible, spend the day as a family eating and giving thanks. Even if the law were changed I honestly believe that the vast majority of Americans would continue to celebrate this holiday. It is a beautiful example of the power and evolution of a culture. Families that were raised with stories of the first Thanksgiving have helped to create and reinforce culture that is passed from generation to generation.

I enjoy using several definitions of culture. The simplest being the way things are done in a particular place by a particular group of people. As Christians, the concept of a people group coping with their world is a great place to start. In the book of Ephesians the Apostle Paul describes us as being seated in heavenly places. This means we are a people group that belongs in heaven but is learning to cope with life on earth. This concept, along with our understanding of being apostolic — sent from heaven to make earth look like heaven — gives a powerful context for culture. Our Christian culture is the way we do things here on earth with a mindset based in heaven.

It may be that the closest we can get to finding the word "culture" in the Bible is the use of the word "nature" in 2 Peter 1:4 where Peter talks about us becoming "partakers of the divine nature." When I read the Bible it is verses like this that are always a combination of challenging, encouraging, and shocking. We are called to imitate Paul as he imitates Christ. We're equally invited by Paul to be imitators of God and partakers of His divine nature. So many Christians are robbed of these invitations because they are led to believe they exist in a sin nature, unredeemed by the fullness of the cross of Jesus Christ. But these verses are inviting us, calling us to the potential we have been given to create and affect culture in our lives on earth.

Culture creates a sense of ownership and it is also defined as the way in which a group of people solve problems. Once again, this points to us as Christian believers. We want to create ownership of what we believe, and we believe our culture is the solution to the world's problems. Christian culture, although having the hallmarks of all of the elements described in organizational culture, has not harnessed its full potential. Organizational culture, as described by Terrence Deal and Allan Kennedy, contains the following phenomena: History, values and beliefs, rituals and ceremonies, stories, heroic figures, and cultural network. This describes the Christian faith globally and also organizationally. This list leads me to believe that the power of culture has not been fully grasped by us as believers.

In the context of organizations, culture is central. Culture is required in order to achieve an organization's vision, fulfill the mission, and prove the structure's success. Understanding culture is, therefore, a powerful resource as an administrator. It is the lens through which everything is viewed and, as such, will affect everything in an organization. One of my favorite examples in this regard is the discussion within the charismatic world of miracles and process. Both are a part of our lives, but the goal of the believer is a culture of miracles that embraces process rather than a culture of process with the occasional miracle. At first glance they may seem the same, but they are radically different and will create very different experiences and outcomes.

There are negative elements to culture which may need addressing. Even cultures that are fundamentally good can develop destructive traits. Likemindedness, narrow-mindedness, and right-mindedness (arrogance) are just a few examples. Culture is an opportunity for every leader. It can indeed be led from the top, but it is influenced and grows from the ground up. Culture needs to be understood, to be nurtured, and every opportunity taken to draw on the strengths available while avoiding the constraints of its weaknesses.

Perhaps most important of all examples is the apostolic assignment to bring the culture of heaven to earth. The origin of the word apostle, as you already know, is from the Romans who sent their military leaders (apostles) to make other places look and behave like Rome. These Roman apostles were sent to make the culture like Rome, and yet Jesus took this very title and applied it to himself and his twelve disciples. While we are not all Apostles, we should be apostolic, having embraced the mindset of believing that we are sent ones to make earth look and behave like heaven. In other words it is culture that we bring and culture that we affect.

Culture is being created all around us. The ease of communication, social media, access to information, and global marketing are a few elements enabling cultures to be created overnight. The age in which we live is far more susceptible to cultural change than any previous age. The globalization of the planet and the ease of communication have brought changes which previously took decades to establish. This is our opportunity to live as believers with these assignments and attributes of a divine nature, to no longer see ourselves as second-class, nor to leave the non-church world to unbelievers. What we have the world needs, and knowing who we are and what we carry is essential to seeing the power of heaven's culture impact the earth.

2

Culture that Overflows

I was sat at a wedding recently. It was a wedding of an old school friend of my wife so I didn't know many people there. As my wife was off talking to some old friends I sat at the edge of the room looking around and suddenly, from nowhere, I was overwhelmed by the lack of freedom and joy that seemed to hover over many people in the room.

There was nothing unusual about these people. They didn't have greater difficulties than anyone one else. Yet God was showing me how many people are captive to their circumstances, to disappointment and discouragement, and the result – a life that isn't all that it could be and isn't redeemed from being empty.

Most of these people weren't Christians, yet the story isn't that different for many Christians. They know where they are going to end up, but all too often their life becomes about survival until they finally reach heaven.

Imagine if you lived in complete freedom. Imagine if all of the people in your church had complete freedom, understood the gifts and calling on their lives and lived life to the fullest. Imagine if everyone in your workplace was thriving, reaching their potential, helping others to do the same and building a lasting legacy.

Imagine that you, your congregation and your colleagues didn't experience fear, worry, discouragement and lack of hope or anything else that stops you from living life to the fullest. As this happens you are transformed into people of beauty, joy, praise and righteousness. You begin to thrive personally. Your church thrives. Your business thrives, and you can't help but for it to also overflow into your communities. Relationships will be rebuilt and people all around you will be restored into who they were created to be. Imagine that through this you gained everlasting joy.

Sounds good doesn't it? Jesus said that this was his purpose here on earth (Is 61:1-7 & Jn 10:10). Jesus is perfect so he must have achieved his purpose. Therefore this must be possible. It must be available for us now.

This book challenges us to raise our expectations to see this in our lives, our churches and our businesses. It offers practical thoughts, ideas and tools, to revive our personal lives, to lead others into this fullness and for this to overflow into the communities we are part of in a sustained way through the culture that we create.

The Quest

The history of the human race is a quest to be revived without knowing that revival is what it is searching for. Individually it takes the forms of hedonism, capitalism, spiritual enlightenment, self-help gurus, greed, sexual exploration and self-obsession. The unspoken cry echoes through the generations: "there must be more than this, there must be something that will fill the empty void, something to plug the hole, and something to create a feeling of wholeness and fullness that lasts and doesn't empty out".

Corporately our organisations of all types; businesses, churches and families are also looking to be revived. Over recent years this search has been given a different name; 'engagement'. The quest to increase engagement or to 'engage our people', is our organisations crying out for revival without knowing that is the answer.

The quest for 'engagement' is a search for something more. The search is advancing. The leaders of this quest have realised that people are unique and what 'engages' one might not engage another. They have realised that people are deep. Logic and rationale only go so far and for most people logic isn't nearly as important and meaningful as our strong emotional drivers.

In essence the leaders of this quest are learning how to understand human nature; the good and the bad and through this understanding are discovering what makes people tick; what engages them, perhaps even what revives them.

However there is a vital piece of the jigsaw missing. The human race is made in the image of God. We might not always look and behave like him, but deep within all of us is a yearning; a craving to become that image again; to be made full.

Jesus said *"I have come that they may have life and have it to the full"* (Jn10:10). He is the answer to this quest. It is through Jesus that each of us can live in the fullness of life and through him that our groups of people; churches, businesses and families achieve all of their hopes, dreams and missions. They become engaged and revived.

It sounds great, but why doesn't it happen more? Perhaps it is understandable why some of our big corporates don't engage people and certainly aren't being revived. After all they function as impersonal profit focussed machines, don't they? What about churches though? They know Jesus and know he came to give life in all its fullness, but are all members of our churches being everything they can be and living in the fullness that Jesus brings? What about you individually? Are you continually living in the fullness? Do you always feel like you are living out the purpose you are here on the planet for?

To receive the fullness that Jesus has for us we need to understand two parts of an equation. The first part is our human nature; the good and the bad, the way God has made us and the rebellion from the fall that creates in us the propensity to do things our own way. The second part is to understand the Kingdom of heaven, how God loves to work with us, in us and through us and what Jesus has done to free us from our rebellion.

People come alive when they are understood. Imagine what could happen if we combined an understanding of people; our human nature, with an understanding of how Jesus came to bring life to all of us. Imagine if we combined new ways of being and of leading people with an invitation for Jesus to enter into these situations. We will live in the fullness that Jesus came to give. This will create revival! People will be revived personally and when this happens it always has to overflow, especially if we create a culture that encourages and facilitates that overflow.

What is engagement?

I am involved in a UK government task force aimed at increasing engagement levels in the workforce so that, as a country, we are more productive and competitive. This is at the coal face of the quest. How can we create cultures where individuals thrive and, as a result, whole organisations, whether it's a church or a business, become more productive and successfully achieve their objectives, goals and dreams?

True engagement comes when there are deep emotional and spiritual connections made; connections that lead people towards fullness of life. When individuals within a group are living life in its fullness, then the group or organisation will also achieve much greater things. When Jesus is at the centre of this; then it is revival.

This book looks at the essence of our human nature to help us understand who we are and the way we tick. It combines this with looking at the way God works in us, with us and through us so that we can be revived personally and, as leaders in church and business, create a culture that revives our organisations so they are functioning at their best, as Jesus intends them to and intends us to.

The book is intentionally structured around the latest research in engagement, motivation and behavioural economics. Studies in these areas highlight our nature. They highlight the way we have been made by our creator and also reflect something of God's character, after all, we are made in our creator's image. When we combine an understanding of who we are, with an understanding of the people we have been created to be and the way God works in us, with us and through us, then we open ourselves up to our good God of love and his empowering presence. This will transform us into the people he created us to be and to live life to the fullest as Jesus came to give us.

The book is for us personally, but it mustn't stop there. It looks to help us all develop cultures of fullness so we can also lead our families, churches and businesses into life as it is meant to be. It is about overflowing with joy, hope and the goodness of God so our communities and cities are transformed into his likeness.

This book looks at creating a culture of fullness in a series of concentric circles. We and our personal cultural paradigm are at the centre. For us to change anything outside of us, we first have to create the culture we wish to see, inside us. The second circle is that of our families and close relationships. To authentically lead others into fullness, it has to be part of our normal way of living. The third circle represents our businesses, churches and other organisations of which we are part. The fourth circle is for the communities we are part of and society more widely. When we, as the body of Christ, live as Jesus intended it will overflow and affect society. This is reformation, when the church becomes the main cultural influence, seeing the kingdom of heaven break out in everyday life.

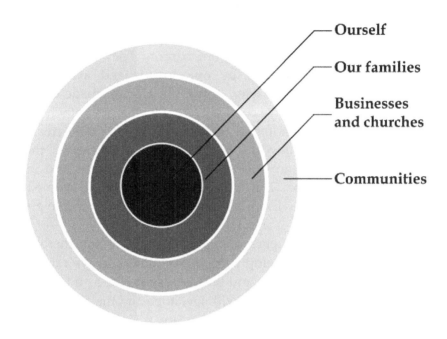

Ourself

Our families

Businesses and churches

Communities

So what about engagement?

Think about Apple geeks (I apologize if you are one of the people I am about to describe) and the deep emotional and possibly spiritual connections they have with the Apple brand. They queue through the night to be one of the first people to get hold of the latest iPhone or iPad. That isn't logical or rational! They could wander into the store a few days later and pick it up without going through the discomfort of queuing through the night on a cold pavement, possibly with rain pouring down on them. They do it because of an incredibly strong emotional engagement to the brand. This emotional engagement is far more powerful than the rational part of them that is saying "don't be stupid, I can get a good night's sleep, stay warm and dry and get my new phone next week"!

Engagement is about these deep heartfelt, emotional and spiritual connections being realized and met. In fact recent research in the field of behavioural economics suggests that for most people, our emotions are a much stronger motivator for decisions and behaviours, than logic and rationale. This has enormous implications for businesses and the church. Most businesses and churches are based on structures and cultures that follow the neo-classical economic view. All this is, is a presumption that we are rational people who make rational decisions. This thinking reflects the predominant cultural view or paradigm, so most people follow it without realising. Most of our management structures, in business and church and much of our leadership training also comes from this view point.

However, it isn't completely true. A few years ago, neuroscientist Antonio Damasio made a ground breaking discovery. He studied people with damage in the part of the brain where emotions are generated. He found that, aside from not being able to feel emotions, they seemed normal. But they all had something peculiar in common: they couldn't make decisions. They could describe what they should be doing in logical terms, yet they found it very difficult to make even simple decisions, such as what to eat.[1]

This discovery showed that our emotions are vital to making decisions, even everyday ones. The more complex a decision, the more important our emotions become and the less important the logic and rationale.

Let's put this to the test. I want you to imagine the following scenario:

You are on your way to the airport to go on a holiday of a lifetime. You are off to the Maldives and you have seen the brochure of where you are going. You will have your own private beach front apartment on a white sandy beach with the waves lapping just in front of your sun kissed terrace. It will be beautifully hot and you can laze about all day if you want, or if you prefer, then there are water sports and adventures to be had. Whatever your dream holiday is you are about to go on it.

You are on the way to the airport and your car breaks down. You call the breakdown services and at this point, there are two different scenarios.

Scenario 1 - the break down service takes about two hours to get to you. They look at your car and can't fix it. You decide to go to the airport anyway just in case your flight has been delayed. They haul your car onto the back of the tow truck and take you to the airport. You push the car into a parking bay, grab your bags and rush through to departures. It isn't much of a surprise for you to find you have missed your flight by two hours.

Scenario 2 – the break down service gets to you remarkably quickly. They look at your car and manage to fix it and get you back on the road. The traffic is really heavy and it's touch and go as to whether you will make the flight or not. You arrive at the airport, park the car, grab your luggage and rush through to departures only to find that you have missed your flight by two minutes.

I want you now to think which of the scenarios would make you more frustrated and you have three options:

- Option 1 – scenario 1, missing the flight by two hours would make you more frustrated
- Option 2 – scenario 2, missing the flight by two minutes would make you more frustrated
- Option 3 – you would be equally frustrated. You missed your flight either way so there would be no difference to your levels of frustration.

Which did you go for? I've used this scenario in workshops with thousands of people and in total, about 70% go for option 2, about 29% go for option 3 and a very small number go for option 1.

The rational answer is option 3. You missed the flight so you've missed it. However for the majority of people it's easier to imagine what it would have been like when you only just miss it, than when you miss it by a long way. This is an emotional response. It's not a wrong response, or a right response, but it's how most of us are wired to think and make decisions.

Good engagement understands these emotional decision making points and 'engages' with people at these points. That's what the best brands do. That's what Apple have managed to do with many of their customers to turn them into an army of advocates that are willing to put themselves through relative discomfort just to get a new product before everyone else. The best organisations also do this with their staff. They engage with their staff at such a deep emotional and sometimes spiritual level that the staff love working there, they feel empowered, happy, and joyful, motivated and go the extra mile for the organisation. This sounds very similar to Isaiah 61.

> ... *to bestow on them a crown of beauty instead of ashes, the oil of joy instead of mourning, and a garment of praise instead of a spirit of despair* (Is 61:3)

When the captives are freed and the prisoners released, look what happens; beauty, joy and praise are created. We will explore that in more depth later!

So if engagement is about our deep heartfelt, emotional and spiritual connections being realized and met and it is also the search for revival without knowing it, then revival is also about us living out the destiny that God has for us. When we do this we are completely fulfilled through the fullness of the relationship with him, with others and through the purpose of our lives.

The cultures of overflow

As part of my work investigating engagement I undertook a comprehensive literature review of all of the main studies in motivation, engagement, behaviour and behavioural economics. I identified eight key areas of emotional decision making that most of the studies agree impact on engagement. Looking at this the other way round; creating a culture that takes account of these areas and builds them into the way we lead, will result in sustained engagement. When this is combined with an invitation to God to move in power in us, with us and through us, then we are moving towards living life to the full as Jesus described. We help people discover who God has made them to be and the purposes that he has for them.

Following is a short summary of the eight areas. In some cases I use several terms for each area because the language we use in a church context and a business context is often so different, although it is actually looking at the same thing. There is a chapter on each of these areas that examines both: our understanding of human nature and explores what the bible says about the way God works with us, in us and through us to turn our human nature into a culture of fullness. It is amazing how similar some of the psychological research and theories are to what the bible says. Although I suppose it perhaps shouldn't be surprising, as the good aspects of us should point towards our heavenly Father as we are made in his image and all good things, whether secular or sacred, come from him.

Each chapter will practically look at what you can do as an individual to develop these areas and turn them into a culture of fullness in your own life and through your leadership, impact on others so they also live life as Jesus intended.

1 Meaning, vision and purpose

How do we create an engaging vision that is breathed on by God? How do we empower others to have their own visions, and support them to live them out, at the same time as seeing ours come to fruition? How do we ensure our visions are as big, deep and long as God's vision for us and our organisations?

2 Being purposeful, conquering our habits

How do we live purposefully so our vision becomes reality? How do we turn our well meaning intentions into reality? How do we develop positive habits and break old ones? How do we intentionally become the people God has created us to be and to do the things he has called us to do through the power of the Holy Spirit and a transformed mind.

3 Overcoming cultural influences

Our minds are influenced by what we feed ourselves with and allow them to dwell on. Our minds in turn influence our emotions which then influence our behaviours. How do we ensure the influences on us are positive and lead us into fullness? How do we create positive cultures in our families, churches and businesses that positively influence others? What do we need to do to survive or indeed thrive in hostile environments that negatively influence us?

4 Self Expectations – knowing our identity and authority

How do we stay true to our identity as sons and daughters of God rather than reduce our expectations of what is possible to the level of a mere mortals without God on their side? Do we understand the authority that we have as children of God and know how to use that authority to see his kingdom come in all spheres of society? How do we help others we lead know their identity and authority?

5 Overcoming loss and fear

Human nature focuses more on preventing loss and maintaining the status quo than on taking risk to achieve possible gain. How can we increase our faith so we see risk through God's eyes and with his wisdom rather than taking a position of fear? How can we increase the power, love and supernatural wisdom in our decision making so the gifts God has given us are realised?

6 Leader's traits - being fathers and mothers

What does it mean to be 'fathers' and 'mothers' to people in a way that encourages them to a sustained place of fullness? What are the personal characteristics of leaders that result in the most engaged, or revived followers and what can we do so these characteristics are more obvious in our lives?

7. Using our strengths to live a full life

Our strengths are God given, but how can we understand the giftings we have and use them more? How can we recognise and develop others in their strengths? How can we use and recognise our strengths but not become self-reliant? What does being poor in spirit have to do with this?

8 Empowering others and creating a legacy

Empowerment is passing power to other people. How can we best empower others to become all they can be? How can we be empowered by previous generations and empower others in generations to come to create a legacy of fullness of life and revival?

References

1. Damasio, A. (2006) *Descartes' Error – Emotion, Reason and the Human Brain,* New York, Penguin.

3

Overflowing with Purpose

When groups of people are engaged or revived they achieve their goals and missions more effectively. So what are our goals and missions? Well each organisation will have their own specific ones, but there are two particular occasions when Jesus gave a commission to his disciples. When the disciples were first sent out Jesus told them to; *"preach this message: 'The kingdom of heaven is near.' Heal the sick, raise the dead, cleanse those who have leprosy, drive out demons"*. (Mt 10:7-8)

Later on in the great commission Jesus said, as his parting words to his disciples before ascending to heaven; *"All authority in heaven and on earth has been given to me. Therefore go and make disciples of all nations, baptising them in the name of the Father and of the Son and of the Holy Spirit and teaching them to obey everything I have commanded you. And surely I am with you always to the very end of the age."* (Mt 28:18-20)

Engagement, or personal revival, is about living in the fullness of who we have been created to be and from this place, fulfilling the mission we have been given. The result of revived and engaged people, whether at church or work, is they fulfil the commission they have been set. For Christians the commission Jesus set is to make earth as it is in heaven. (Mt 6:10) This applies to our families, churches, businesses and the communities and cultures we are part of.

This book explores what it means to live life in all its fullness and how, as leaders, we can develop a culture of fullness in our churches and businesses, so that each individual is fulfilling their potential and living the life they were always meant to live. As a result, each organisation or church will be far more effective at delivering the mission they have been set and will also overflow beyond its immediate context and into the community. That means we should expect to see the sick healed, the dead raised, people set free and nations discipled, both in church and out of church.

Three times of personal revival

Reflecting back on my life so far I think there are three particular times or events when I have experienced a personal revival. One of these was fairly short lived and the other two are still on-going.

I will share these three events with you as mini case studies to try and communicate the essence of full life that I experienced in these times. As you read them, think about times when you have also experienced your own personal revivals.

By that, I mean times when you felt particularly aligned to the plans and purposes that God has for you, and as a result, moved above the mundane and the normal to achieve the extraordinary. I use the word 'achieve' loosely, as the plans and purposes that God has for you, at a particular time, may be more to do with learning about him and resting in his presence than actually 'achieving' something in the human sense of the word.

Saturday Night Service

The first of these times of personal revival came when I was 17. It was the summer of my A Levels and suddenly, in about May time, I felt a prompting by the Holy Spirit to start a Saturday night church service. Some might say that it was just procrastination and a good 'spiritual' way to avoid doing the revision I should have been doing, but it wasn't. It was more than that.

I was a good Christian boy, with fantastic Christian parents and I'd always known Jesus as my Lord and Saviour. However, out of the blue and completely contrary to anything I'd done before, I felt an urge to run this service. I wasn't praying any more than usual and hadn't been to a charismatic event that either hyped me into doing something or empowered me through the Holy Spirit to do something. No, just in my normal day to day I felt an urge to do this.

I gathered a few of my friends and together we set up these services, running every Saturday night from the middle of May to the middle of September, when I went off to university. Part of the prompting I felt was the importance of unity between the churches. So I got on the phone to every church leader of all denominations in Rugby, where I lived, and the surrounding area, and asked if I could come and see them and tell them about what we were doing. Maybe because we were just an enthusiastic bunch of teenagers they pretty much all said yes. So we turned up with flyers already printed ready for them to hand out to their congregations, and a whole load of passion and energy.

The services were about 45 minutes of worship followed by a 15 – 20 minute, very rough and ready, talk by one of us. After about the third week we started to take anyone who was interested into the town centre to prayer walk and evangelise to those leaving pubs and going into clubs.

The nights were really successful. Many of the church leaders advertised them to their congregations and we had good numbers. In fact one week we were overflowing because the whole of a mission team from Bethel Church in Redding California also came along and certainly helped to notch things up a level or two.

I felt alive during this time. Nothing seemed hard or difficult. It just flowed. It was certainly exciting seeing what

God was doing, but more than that, it was as if my energy and motivation came from a deep down subconscious feeling that, what I was doing was completely aligned with God's purposes for me at that time.

In mid-September I left Rugby to go to university in Newcastle and the service finished. What also finished and wasn't to restart in the same way until 14 years later, was the same sense of alignment, purpose, energy and motivation. That's not to say I had some sort of crisis. I didn't. I got really involved in church, playing rugby and university life. I started a nightclub ministry and helped to produce and record an album in a young offender's institute. I took a year out with Youth for Christ after university and then went into marketing and eventually management consultancy. All of this was good. There was purpose behind it, and I don't think I was rebelling from God's will in any of it. However there is a difference between the 'good' that I have just described and the 'great' feeling of real life that I experienced during that A Level summer.

What led to that feeling of real life? Why did it go? My aim is to examine these moments of fullness so we can learn how to live in this state constantly and develop cultures in our organisations, churches and families that create and sustain this for all people.

My healing story

The second time I experienced this sense of personal revival started in very difficult circumstances. In March 2012 I was on holiday with my wife Holly and my two young girls. I had a flu like virus that I tried to be brave about so as not to get accused of having 'man flu'. Gradually I started losing control of my fingers and the muscles in my legs and stomach began to really hurt. We got home at the end of the holiday and it continued to get worse. The loss of control and feeling in my fingers spread up my arms and started in my feet, before moving up my legs as well. I remember being asked to sign a form for my daughter's swimming lessons and I literally couldn't grip the pen.

I didn't go to the doctors straight away. I think I knew it was something serious and I would end up in hospital. Holly and I had promised to host a quiz night for our neighbour's daughter who was raising money to climb Mt. Kilimanjaro. I'm not sure how I managed to drive home after the quiz. The only way I could use the clutch was to haul my left leg upwards with my arms!

The next day was a Sunday and by this stage I couldn't really walk or use my arms. I went to the out of hours GP who sent me straight to hospital. The male assessment ward was full so I was put in a private room on the women's assessment ward. They undertook various tests and diagnosed me as having Transverse Myelitis (TM). I didn't know what it was and the Doctors didn't explain much there and then, but my initial reaction was relief as I thought that, now there was a diagnosis, the doctors would be able to treat it. Holly asked them how long I would be in hospital and they avoided the question in a very jovial manner.

Holly then had to leave to move our children from one kind person looking after them to another. As she left she saw the Doctors at the other end of the corridor. She asked them for a bit more detail about when I would be out as we had small kids and she needed to make plans. Again they were quite evasive so she said to them; "Will he be home by Easter?"

Easter was still two weeks away and seemed a long way off.

"No definitely not" was the doctors' reply.

Becoming increasingly concerned Holly then asked; "Will he be home by our daughters second birthday on May 7th?"

This was a full six weeks away. Her question was met by the same response, "No, definitely not." The doctors then told her to make plans for me being in hospital for months at the minimum and to start thinking about selling our house and getting a bungalow for mobility reasons as I may never be able to move properly again.

At the same time, inside my hospital room, I was just about managing to google the condition on my phone by typing with my thumb, which was about all that stuck out of my now curled over hand. I read some horrendous statistics that were later confirmed by the doctor. Around 90% of people with TM end up with a permanent disability or paralysis, and the 10% who do get better are often left with low levels of disability and take months to recover. It is caused by the immune system attacking the spinal cord and causing swelling. Doctors keep you in hospital until symptoms plateau and in my case, because the swelling was high up the spinal cord, that meant staying in hospital ready to put me on a respirator in case I lost control of the muscles in my chest and lungs.

Needless to say we were both filled with fear. I was young! What about the rest of my life? I was the sole bread winner as Holly stayed at home looking after the children. What would happen to our mortgage? I was the Commercial Director of a small management consultancy who certainly couldn't afford to pay me generous sick leave for an indefinite period. I also worried whether they would survive without me, as I was responsible for bringing in a fair proportion of the work?

We contacted as many people in our church and any other Christian friends we could think of, to pray. Holly and my two daughters, Olivia and Beatrice, all prayed for me in my hospital bed, as did my Pastor, Craig Deal, who dropped everything and came to the hospital. One other close friend also came to the hospital that evening to pray for me. Whilst JJ Waters was in the hospital car park he felt a real oppression, but also felt he heard God tell him to command me to pick up my bed and walk. He also felt God say that I would be preaching the following Sunday; sharing testimony of a miraculous healing. Now for most people this would create all sorts of mixed feelings of; 'what if I say it and it doesn't happen' or 'what will people think of me' or even 'will Dave be cross with me'. However JJ still faithfully shared with me what he felt God was saying. What JJ didn't know is I was actually scheduled to be preaching at church the following Sunday anyway, something that turned into an incredible opportunity to give glory to God for the miraculous way in which I was healed. JJ possibly has the loudest voice of anyone I know, so as he was praying for me and commanding me to pick up my bed and walk I could hear comments from the nurses even though I was in a private room!

As JJ prayed I felt something change, not in my body, but in my spirit. It's hard to explain but I suddenly felt the urge to take ownership for my healing and to take authority over the illness. As a result my faith increased and peace flowed into my body. I wasn't healed there and then. In fact, during the night it got worse. I was pretty much paralysed from my neck downwards and had to call nurses at three points during the night to roll me over because I couldn't do it myself.

At some point during the night I must have drifted off to sleep as when I woke up I was healed! I got out of bed, which I hadn't been able to do before, went to the toilet, and actually got dressed. I stayed in hospital for another day to have further MRI scans, all of which conclusively proved that I had TM but overnight it left my body, something that the doctors had no explanation for!

Experiencing God's love and power in such a personal way led me pretty quickly to another of these personal revival moments. I knew beyond doubt that God had a plan and a purpose for our lives. I also knew beyond doubt that He is a God of immense love and immense power and that the plans of the enemy to steal, kill and destroy (Jn 10:10) pale into insignificance in comparison to God's love, promises and purpose.

We didn't know what the plans and purposes were. However the journey since then, of drawing closer to him and finding teaching that explained the healing I had experienced and the feelings of closeness to God we were also now experiencing, has in itself been an experience of living in fullness, where the purpose we have is energizing, exciting and motivating.

Inventing DEEP

The third example of these periods of personal revival is very different. Or at least, it seems to be on the surface. I have had a long held interest and passion for people in the workplace. As a management consultant I spent many long weeks helping organisations of all types become more effective and efficient by streamlining systems and processes. On paper the results were often great; however the reality often didn't seem to match the theory. This isn't because we didn't do our job well. Quite the contrary, we quickly developed a reputation within our client group of being very good in our field. What I realised is that you can improve and streamline a system or process as much as you want, but it is only ever as good as the people who are working within that process.

This led me into further thinking and research about the people. What is it that makes people behave the way that they do? Combined with this was a growing dissatisfaction with the corporate system. The vast majority of people we encountered on consulting assignments were merely 'surviving'. They had little purpose and certainly weren't living in the fullness of life whilst at work. Seeing that work takes up the majority of our lives, to me that meant they weren't living in the fullness of life, 'full stop'.

Eventually I decided to try and do something about it. I undertook a large literature review of any academic work I could find in the fields of motivation, behaviour change, engagement, behavioural economics and many other areas. From this I developed two models. The first is a distilled version of what really matters or what really makes someone engaged, as outlined in chapter 1. The academics used different terms and had some slight differences and I brought these together to identify eight cultures of engagement that seemed to be important and over which there was broad agreement. I also noticed a growing body of evidence that showed a clear link between engagement and productivity. There were quite a few variables at play, but drawing on my rusty A Level maths to begin with and then later, on the assistance of two Cambridge mathematician friends, I created an algorithm that measured how engaged people were. It also then answered the essential question; the impact engagement has on productivity and therefore the return on investment an organisation will see if they engage their staff more.

Now this may be boring to some of you who aren't involved in the corporate world, but it was actually described as 'the golden bullet' by one HR Director. The age old problem for those working with people in organisations is to prove the impact the work has on the bottom line. This has become even more apparent over the last few years as budgets have tightened, cuts have been made and Finance Directors have gained more power. The model that I created now enabled an organisation to see clearly the impact their 'people initiatives' were having and invest in the right areas.

I turned this research into an online tool called DEEP with associated consultancy support and spun it off under a different brand name, separate from the main management consultancy I worked for to keep the brand messages clear. We didn't want to be seen as jacks of all trades and masters of none!

The process of research through to development was another one of these moments of personal revival. I felt alive, I had a clear purpose and the energy and motivation was real. I was sure God was in the process as throughout the development of the models I prayed constantly for inspiration and on numerous occasions was woken up in the night with the answer.

So what is engagement and how does it relate to revival?

I've mentioned a bit about engagement and how I think it is the search for revival, so I probably need to expand on that a little bit more. Isaiah 61 is that famous passage that Jesus said he fulfilled at the beginning of his ministry. This is a great illustration of what revival is and what engagement is searching for. Have a look at the first seven verses below and think of it in terms of yourself individually, of your church and your workplace.

> *The Spirit of the Sovereign Lord is on me, because the Lord has anointed me to proclaim good news to the poor. He has sent me to bind up the broken-hearted, to proclaim freedom for the captives and release from darkness for the prisoners,[2] to proclaim the year of the Lord's favour and the day of vengeance of our God, to comfort all who mourn, [3] and provide for those who grieve in Zion –to bestow on them a crown of beauty instead of ashes, the oil of joy instead of mourning, and a garment of praise instead of a spirit of despair. They will be called oaks of righteousness,*
> *a planting of the Lord for the display of his splendour.*
> *[4] They will rebuild the ancient ruins and restore the places long devastated;they will renew the ruined cities that have been devastated for generations. [5] Strangers will shepherd your flocks; foreigners will work your fields and vineyards. [6] And you will be called priests of the Lord, you will be named ministers of our God.*
> *You will feed on the wealth of nations, and in their riches you will boast. [7] Instead of your shame you will receive a double portion, and instead of disgrace you will rejoice in your inheritance. And so you will inherit a double portion in your land, and everlasting joy will be yours.*

How many of you or your colleagues, friends or family feel poor, broken-hearted or captive? Through my work with big corporates, I'd say the majority of the workforce are captives. They survive in order to pay their bills but they don't thrive. They don't live as the people God has created them to be and if they do, they probably do it in their church setting, creating a clear divide between church and work.

I think the same can be said for many churches. Maybe people aren't captives, but all too often, they are not living in the fullness of Christ and experiencing the beauty, joy and praise described in verse 3.

What about thinking about our own individual setting rather than our church or workplace? Are we truly free? Are we expecting to continually experience beauty, joy and praise? Jesus came to fulfil this prophecy and sent the Holy Spirit to give us this freedom (2 Cor 3:17). Surely we now should be experiencing all of the blessings that are described here?

This is a picture of fullness. This is what engagement is searching for. It is what the human race has been on a quest to find since the beginning of time. Jesus is saying he meets people where they are at; poor, broken hearted and captive, and he transforms them into people of beauty, joy, praise and righteousness. Amazing, but look what happens next, the year of the Lord's favour is proclaimed and these poor, broken hearted captives are transformed into people who rebuild the ancient ruins, renew the ruined cities, and are called priests of the Lord. They receive a double portion from the Lord and have everlasting joy.

Wow. I'm sure most of you have read that before, but think of it from a workplace perspective. Most workforces are largely surviving; many people are captive to the corporate system and are staying only because they have bills to pay and mouths to feed. Jesus came to set them free. Jesus came that they can live life to the fullest at work as well as in church and in their own personal lives. When they are set free the year of the Lord's favour is proclaimed (Is 61:2). When a workforce is engaged, productivity increases dramatically – the Lord's favour. When people are revived, it will be the year of the Lord's favour for their communities as they overflow with his love and blessings.

The workers who were captive to the system then become producers. They become the people going out and rebuilding, finding more lost people and bringing the kingdom of heaven to the world.

This is engagement in action; each individual person having a personal revival so they are set free from captivity and bondage and released into a new purpose. This purpose not only fulfils them as a person, but has a heavenly impact as they start releasing the kingdom of heaven into the context of their everyday lives.

The same applies in the church. What percentage of a church's congregation are consumers and what are producers? Of those that are producers, are they producing in a way that is purely serving someone else's vision or are they able to use all of the skills and gifts they have been given, growing in them further and living a life fulfilling the potential and destiny that Jesus has for them? I'm not saying there is anything wrong with serving. Far from it, we are called to serve. However, in many churches there is a real divide between the professionals, the priesthood, and the rest. When this divide happens, even if it is sub-conscious and unintentional, the affect is often that the main body of the congregation only serve and don't develop their giftings, skills, calling and passions. In effect, they don't live in the fullness of life.

I think this is why Jesus said; "I will build my church" (Mt 16:18). He knew that when 'we' build it, the focus will be on achieving the vision of the leader. By definition, everyone else then has to service this vision and never get their own. They never truly become the people God created them to be and live life to the full. By contrast, what we have been told to do is to make disciples. This doesn't stop when someone has been a Christian for a week, a month, a year or in fact ever. We are always experiencing new depths of Christ's love for us. We are not called to make big churches. We are called to make big people. That has to be our focus. Interesting though, when building big people is our focus, big and successful churches and businesses often follow.

This book isn't just for church leaders. It is for those 'in ministry' in the church and for those 'in ministry' in the workplace. Jesus didn't differentiate between these groups when he showed the kingdom of heaven in action here on earth and therefore neither should we.

Church has consciously and subconsciously taught us that there are ministry leaders and the role of the rest of us is to support them and their vision financially and in action. We have then taken this model and applied it in the world. We have created organisations with a leader at the top with everyone else a servant to their vision. It could even be argued, and I have seen this case made many times, that actually the church is following the pattern of leadership modelled by the corporate world. There is a leader at the top and everyone else serves them.

Jesus came to bring life to all, not just to the leaders. He came to give all of us vision and purpose, not just leaders. He made all of us part of the royal priesthood, not just the Levites as it was in the Old Testament.

The next chapters look at what it means for us all to live life in all its fullness and to lead others in such a way so they are too. This should be in all walks of life; at work, in church, in our families and in our communities. In Peter's first letter he reminds the readers that they are *redeemed from the empty way of life from your ancestors* (1 Pt 1:18). If we have been redeemed from an empty way of life then being full to overflowing should be normal.

The bible tells us to 'seek first the kingdom of God' (Mt 6:33) and we are told to pray that earth becomes like heaven (Mt 6:10). We are also told to heal the sick, cast out demons, raise the dead and cleanse lepers (Mt 10:7,8). At no point does the bible say; 'but only when you are in church' or even; 'but only when you are with others from church and doing it on the streets'. No, we are told to do these things full stop in whatever context we live our lives.

Paul, in his letter to the Colossians, wrote; 'and whatever you do [no matter what it is] in word or deed, do everything in the name of Jesus and in [dependence upon] his Person, giving praise to God the Father through him (Col 3:17 Amplified Bible).

This says whatever we do, do it with complete dependence on him and do it in the name of Jesus. This therefore must include our everyday work. Especially when considering we spend more time at work that anywhere else.

In biblical times there weren't large corporates and organisations as there are now, except perhaps the armies. Maybe we can liken our modern day corporations to Jericho, Nineveh or Antioch. They are the mission grounds that we are in and have been called to be in through the name of Jesus, depending upon his person for everything we do there.

What we do in the church is not more important than this. In fact what we do in the church should support, empower and equip us to go into our workplaces, in the power of the Holy Spirit, to proclaim the kingdom of heaven is at hand and to heal the sick, cast out demons, raise the dead and cleanse lepers.

Recently Jon Foreman, singer with the band Switchfoot was asked if they were a 'Christian' band. I love his response:

"Does Lewis or Tolkien mention Christ in any of their fictional series? Are Bach's sonata's Christian? What is more Christ-like, feeding the poor, making furniture, cleaning bathrooms or painting a sunset? There is a schism between the sacred and the secular in all our modern minds. The view that a pastor is more 'Christian' than a girls' volleyball coach is flawed and heretical. The stance that a worship leader is more spiritual than a janitor is condescending and flawed"[1]

In the New Testament, Stephen gives us a brilliant description of what it means and looks like to see the kingdom of heaven come to our everyday work situation. He was chosen to feed the widows of an ethnic minority group because it was taking up too much of the Apostle's time as they were called to preach the gospel (Acts 6:4). Stephen did this practical and possibly mundane task, through the power of the Holy Spirit and signs, wonders and miracles were such a normal occurrence that he became known for this (Acts 6:8). He didn't see his work as different from the apostles. He saw his work as an opportunity to fulfil the same commission that the apostles had, just in a different context.

It is for this reason that this book is purposely drawing on secular academic studies and the bible. God is good and all good things come from him (Jam1:17), so where an academic study has identified something useful and helpful and it backs up what the bible says, then I think it makes perfect sense for us to use it as a tool to help us understand more about the way people operate and the plans and purposes God has for us as individuals and for the organisations we lead.

References
1. Quoted in www.faithlikes.com/2014/04/05/this-is-why-switchfoot-wont-sing-christian-songs-anymore.

4

Meaning, Vision and Purpose

Deriving a sense of purpose in what we do and why we do it is so important. Finding meaning and having a vision that we are working towards motivates us and often gives us the strength to keep on going, even if things seem tough. Learning to live in a meaningful and purposeful way with a vision inspiring us and guiding us on is the first of the eight areas of engagement we are exploring.

When we see an alignment between our values and the formal and informal values of the groups, families, businesses and churches we are involved with, then we are engaged, motivated and brought into life.

To illustrate this point let's look at two very different approaches to evangelism that churches typically take. One goes out onto the streets, introduces people to Jesus through an encounter with the love and power of the Holy Spirit and then invites these people to church so they can become part of a community of believers. They train their congregations to all do this so it becomes part of the normal life of the church.

The other approach invites people to church with the hope that they meet Jesus whilst at church. They encourage the congregation to invite people to church and then to leave the gospel message to the people running the service. Now I'm not saying one is right and the other wrong as both see fruit. However the first approach feels somehow so much more meaningful to me. I have values around empowering the whole congregation to do the work and to be the people they were created to be (the subject of this book!) and around the church extending the kingdom into all areas of society. The first model of evangelism aligns with my values and the impact of it is exciting and motivating to me! Truth be told, the second approach actually affects me in the opposite way. Although I hope and pray it will also bear fruit, I easily feel disconnected, constrained and frustrated.

Now I haven't written this to make a point about the right way to do evangelism, but to demonstrate the motivational impact an alignment of values has.

This alignment, or lack of alignment, is important to think about before considering what vision is, because our visions can either bring people to life, like the first example, or have the opposite effect.

Have you ever been in a situation where what you were hearing and seeing was so different to your experiences that it actually made you feel stressed? A slightly harder question to answer, because it happens in a more subtle way is; have you ever noticed yourself creating justifications to explain things that are at odds with your experiences? On reflection have you noticed that the justifications are more unbelievable than the original event you are trying to justify?

I saw an example of this when I was healed of Transverse Myelitis. What the Doctors were seeing was very definitely at odds with their experiences! Their experiences were of a continued deterioration for a period of time, disability and lengthy hospital stays. Their experiences were at complete odds with my waking up healed the next morning.

This caused them a very noticeable level of discomfort and

they tried very hard to create justifications for what had happened. These justifications centred on the idea that the wrong diagnosis must have been given in the first instance. They developed many theories as to what had been wrong with me, all of which they had ruled out earlier because they didn't match with my symptoms or the results of the MRI scans. Their justifications were becoming more far fetched than the reality which was that God had healed me!

A really interesting piece of work was undertaken by Leon Festinger[1] in the 1950s that explains these natural human reactions. His work, the theory of cognitive dissonance, showed that humans strive for internal consistency. When inconsistency (dissonance) is experienced, individuals can become psychologically distressed, or stressed as we would call it. His work led him to two key hypotheses:

- "The existence of dissonance (inconsistency with experiences and world view), being psychologically uncomfortable, will motivate the person to try to reduce the dissonance and achieve consonance"
- "When dissonance is present, in addition to trying to reduce it, the person will actively avoid situations and information which would likely increase the dissonance"

This means we find experiences that are at odds with our previous experiences and expectations stressful and try to avoid them.

He also found that the amount of dissonance, or inconsistency, and the subsequent stress is dependent on an interesting variable:

- *The importance*: The more the experience is valued, the greater the dissonance and stress.

This means that 'dissonance' or stress is particularly prevalent when the event we are experiencing is at odds with something that we value. An example of this would be someone who had very strong environmental values working at an unethical mining company whose inherent values were to exploit the environment. The values of the individual would be so different to the formal and particularly informal values of the mining company, thus creating inconsistency and leading to high levels of stress.

The work my firm and others have done in the field of engagement has demonstrated the impact of alignment of values. The meaning and purpose a person has, and in particular the alignment to the formal and informal values, purpose and vision of the organisation the person is a part of, has a large impact on how engaged someone is and therefore the fullness of life they experience whilst at work. Dan Pink, in his excellent book Drive[2], came to the same conclusion. He identified three factors that influence our intrinsic motivation; autonomy, mastery and purpose. His definition of purpose is very similar to this. He found that we need to have a purpose and we need to see an alignment between that purpose and what we are actually doing at work, in church or in our family and social groups in order to be motivated.

This is why vision is so important: people having a vision and purpose is motivational and brings people alive. We need a vision and we need to lead others in a way so they develop their own vision. When we lead people in businesses and churches we also need to realise the impact our vision and underlying values have on those around us. If they are different from their experiences, expectations and values it actually creates dissonance for them, or as we would commonly experience it; stress.

Festinger's theory is also based on an assumption that people seek consistency between their expectations and reality. Because of this, people engage in a process called dissonance reduction to bring their thoughts, expectations and actions in line with one another. This creation of uniformity allows for less stress.

This reduction can happen in four different ways. Let's have a look at how this plays out in an everyday situation:

Imagine you decided to go on a diet and you are going to avoid high fat foods; however you are in a supermarket and you smell some freshly cooked doughnuts. You buy a doughnut and eat it. There is an immediate dissonance there; you plan to avoid fatty foods but you find yourself eating a doughnut. The four ways we can reduce this dissonance are as follows:

1. Change our behaviour - we stop eating the doughnut remembering how important it is that we avoid fatty foods.
2. Justify behaviour by changing the conditions - "I'm allowed to eat a doughnut once in a while."
3. Justify behaviour by adding new conditions - "I'll spend 30 extra minutes at the gym to work it off."
4. Ignore/deny any information that conflicts with existing beliefs -"I did not eat that doughnut. I always eat healthily."

Which one of these four reactions do you find yourself falling into? Knowing the way our minds work is important so that we can purposefully operate, think and act in the way we want to, not the way we end up doing. I think most of us have tendencies to one or more of these reactions and our tendency is often a learnt behaviour from our childhood.

The same applies to me when sharing my faith with strangers. I have the expressed intention of sharing my faith but all too often I find myself justifying not doing it in a million and one different ways. I normally find myself justifying it by thinking; 'they look really busy so I will actually be making their life more stressful if I try and share my faith with them now, so I won't at the moment'.

The reason I've started this chapter on vision and purpose with this look at cognitive dissonance is because it is so important to understand the impact our vision and values have on those we lead. It is also useful to understand why we react to situations in the way that we do.

The need to have consistency between our experiences and expectations and the reality in which we live, is one of the main reasons for divisions in the church. Over time our theology changes to explain our experiences because we can't cope with the dissonance. For example over many centuries in the church, a school of thinking has developed saying that miracles don't often happen and if they do it is normally only in Africa. I'm perhaps being quite trite with this example but I'm sure you recognise the thought pattern. Theological thinking then begins to back this up, lowering expectations for seeing any miracles. This then removes any dissonance potentially created by reading in the bible that we will perform greater works than Jesus and not seeing any sign of his power working through us in reality. Understanding this powerful effect of the human mind allows us to lead in a way that builds unity, empowers others into their own vision and ultimately glorifies God through people living a full life, with expectations based on the word of God, not our experiences.

If our vision and values are at odds with the personal vision and values of those we lead it will create a dissonance in them that they will react to in different ways. However if we can lead in a way that empowers them into their own vision, helps them grasp God's expectations and creates hope that the reality in which they are living will match these expectations, then we are developing a culture for them to live a full life and move towards revival.

What is vision?

Vision is seeing the future that you are working towards before it is a reality. It is a bridge between the present and the future. A metaphor for vision and change that I often use in workshops is the story of the Oregon Trail.

The Oregon Trail migration is one of the most important events in American History. The Oregon Trail was a 2,170 mile route from Missouri to Oregon and California that enabled the migration of the early pioneers to the western United States. The first emigrants to make the trip were Marcus and Narcissa Whitman who made the journey in 1836. However, the first mass migration did not occur until 1843 when approximately 1000 pioneers made the journey at one time.

This trail was the only feasible land route for settlers to get to the West Coast. From 1843 until 1869 when the first transcontinental railroad was completed, there were over 500,000 people who made the trip in covered wagons pulled by mule and oxen. Some went all the way to Oregon to farm and others went to California to search for gold. The trip usually took 4-6 months by wagon traveling 15 miles a day. The only other route to the west, by sea, took a full year.

Stories from the early fur trappers and missionaries came back to the east coast and the mid-west of just how good the agricultural land was, how much space there was and the riches that were possible by moving to Oregon. Later on, after gold was discovered in California in 1848, stories of great wealth also came back.

Those who set out on the Oregon Trail had a clear vision of the future; that of a better life and great wealth. It was this vision that would keep them going through all of the hardship that they would doubtless face whilst undertaking such a mammoth journey.

In the early spring, emigrant campers would congregate around Independence, Missouri and set up camp, waiting for the grass to grow along the Oregon Trail. While waiting, the emigrants would stock up on supplies, try to locate friends, and make other preparations for their journey. If they left too early there would be no grass for their animals to eat which could be a fatal mistake. If they left too late they would get caught by the winter snows.

Most settlers travelled in farm wagons, four feet by ten feet, with a thousand pounds of food. These wagons had cotton covers treated with linseed oil to keep the rain out. Many were equipped with tool boxes, water containers, and spare axles. A broken axle on the rough trail was not an uncommon occurrence and without a spare it would mean having to abandon the wagon.

When the time finally came to leave, the settlers would all try to leave at once creating a massive traffic jam. This was further hindered by the inexperience and slow progress of some of the east coast teams. As their traveling progressed, most realised they had over packed and were forced to lighten their loads by discarding belongings and provisions along the way. Because of the heavy loads, many were forced to walk the 2,170 mile journey instead of ride in the wagon.

Imagine turning up in Independence Missouri having already left many of your possessions behind, only to find that you had to get rid of even more to make the journey because either they wouldn't fit in the wagon or it made the wagons too heavy. The vision of the future had to be strong to keep people going through the emotional and practical challenges this would have caused.

There were many accidents along the way. Getting run over by one of the wagons resulted in almost certain death for the unfortunate settler. Wounds from accidental gun shots were an all too common occurrence due to people falling around or from half-cocked pistols in the wagons. Another problem for the travellers was Cholera. Some wagon trains lost two-thirds of their people to this quick killing disease. Bodies were usually left on the side of the road or buried in shallow graves which allowed animals to dig them up and scatter their bones along the trail. This proved to be very unnerving for many of the pioneers. Again, the vision of the future had to be strong to keep people going, and even to start out in the first instance with these stories of adversity and tragedy getting back to those who were yet to commence their journeys.

A major danger to the settlers was weather. Traveling in the summer meant dealing with thunder storms, lightening and hail. Many were killed by lightning or hail the size of baseballs. All in all, one in ten did not survive the journey.

The final third of the trail was the most difficult and had to be done with expediency. Winter snows would close the mountain passes and travel was a race against time. In the early years, before the Barlow Road was opened, travellers would have to abandon their wagons for boats and float down the Columbia River. Many lost their lives in the rapids and rough parts just miles from their destination. After 1846, and upon paying a toll, the pioneers could finish their journey by crossing the Cascades on the Barlow Road.

Once in Oregon and California, settlers would start a new life and build farms or set off to the gold mines.

The vision of the future that the early travellers had was what kept them going through the hardship and what encouraged them to make the sacrifice in the first place. The strength of the vision had to be compelling enough for them to endure the hardship and risk which they knew they would likely encounter on the way. The size of the vision determines the sacrifice that people will make.

For these pioneers the vision was long term. People had a vision for their whole lives being changed, not just for a bit of a difference for the next couple of years. The long term nature of their visions had a large impact on their willingness to sacrifice in order to achieve it.

Vision must be strong before strategy is created. By that I mean we must know the 'why' and the 'what' before we start to think about the 'how'. Many times I've worked with organisations that have inhibited their vision by starting to think about how something can be achieved. This shrinks our vision and ultimately makes it less compelling. Do you think those travellers along the Oregon Trail would have bothered if the vision was of a *slightly* better life?

Where does vision come from?

A lot of my work recently has been helping 'strategic planning' teams develop their 'strategic thinking'. There is a subtle yet fundamental difference between the two. Strategic thinking is looking ahead into the future to think about the 'why' and the 'what' questions whilst strategic planning focuses on 'how' we get there. Most organisations are very good at the planning but pretty bad at the thinking. This is because strategic planning is much easier and more comfortable. It is typically short term, logical, pragmatic and creates alignment between different strands of thinking. Strategic thinking, on the other hand, is much more difficult and uncomfortable. It is typically much longer term, uncertain, divergent and incomplete. However it is exactly this type of thinking that is needed to develop the type of compelling vision that people will endure personal sacrifice to follow.

To encourage strategic thinking and the creation of long term vision I encourage teams to think big, deep and long. Thinking in this way is useful whatever type of vision we are creating.

Thinking big

All too often we think too small and our visions are too small. Thinking and dreaming big isn't to be confused with needing everything big straight away. The prophet Zechariah warned against despising the day of small things (Zech 4:10). We need to be content with small beginnings and what God is doing with us and through us in the present. However we need to dream big because God's plans are big. Jesus taught us through many of the parables that the Kingdom of Heaven is always increasing and that we are to steward that increase. This means that what we dream for and have vision for must be greater than seems possible now.

I was recently at a conference at Causeway Coast Vineyard in Northern Ireland. They told us a story of how, at the beginning of 2014, they commissioned three evangelists to each see one person come to faith every day that year. The reply from Mark Marx, one of those evangelists, was 'why only one'? He had vision beyond the possible to territory that seemed to be impossible based on previous experience. Vision limited to what has been, is settling for far less that God plans, hopes for and achieves. Well over 2000 people came to faith through these evangelists in 2014, far exceeding the one a day target and proving Mark Marx right in his understanding of our abundant Father.

A church in Norwich, where I live, has recently been refreshed by a partnership with Holy Trinity Brompton (HTB) in London. The two church leaders, Ian Dyble and Dave Lloyd wrote out a five year vision for the church prior to starting. Eighteen months into the plant they have just moved on to year five of the vision! Their vision was smaller than God's. Ian and Dave have quickly adapted and are a wonderful example of thinking and dreaming big to see the Kingdom of Heaven come here on earth.

Part of thinking big is seeing beyond our own organisation to the wider systems we are part of. This is true in business and church contexts. We need to understand the impact others have on us and the impact we can also have on others. For churches this has got to mean looking beyond our own congregations to what God is doing in our cities. What can we get involved with, how can we bless other churches, how can we be a unified body of Christ that develops this 'big' thinking into our congregations? After all Jesus said it is when the world sees a united church that they will know who God is (Jn 17:21).

Our imaginations and dreams are a wonderful gift from God. He is a creative God who has also made us creative as we are made in his likeness. Too often we can be harsh on our 'dreaming' because culture, particularly in the workplace, tells us to focus more on reality than 'pie in the sky' ideas. We need to reclaim our imaginations for God. We need to ask him to co-imagine and co-dream with us. This is real strategic thinking. Looking ahead, beyond the possible to the realms of impossible that God wants us to move into and inherit. This only works if we then rely on him in accomplishing the vision rather than on our own strength. God infused vision is the starting place for living a revived life of purpose.

Thinking deep

We make assumptions all of the time and these assumptions have a large impact on the decisions that we make, our expectations for what we will achieve and what is possible naturally and supernaturally. Our assumptions are usually based on our past experiences. As such, these assumptions can often encase us in the past, whereby we view the world through a particular lens that is shaded by the different experiences we have had. We often don't realise our lens is shaded, or even sometimes scratched, and therefore don't realise the assumptions we are making.

When developing vision it is really important to identify the assumptions that are impacting on our thinking. The assumptions might prove to be right, but never the less, understanding they are assumptions and not necessarily reality, is very important. A good test to identify the assumptions you are making is to reflect back on times when you've had an idea or someone has put an idea to you and you've thought; 'that won't work', 'that's a crazy idea' or 'I couldn't do that'. When you've identified times like this then try and identify what the assumptions are that are underpinning your reaction. Often the assumptions are also linked to our thoughts about ourselves such as; 'I'm not that good', 'things that good never happen to me' etc. A great book for looking at this in more detail is Steve Backlund's book 'Let's just laugh at that'[3]

In Ephesians Paul prayed:

> *I pray that the eyes of your heart may be enlightened in order that you may know the hope to which he has called you, the riches of his glorious inheritance in his holy people, and his incomparably great power for us who believe. That power is the same as the mighty strength he exerted when he raised Christ from the dead and seated him at his right hand in the heavenly realms, far above all rule and authority, power and dominion, and every name that is invoked, not only in the present age but also in the one to come* (Eph 1:18-21).

By using the term; 'the eyes of your heart' Paul is showing that we actually see with our hearts. The information comes in through our eyes but we interpret this information and see and create vision in our hearts. He is praying that the Ephesians' hearts would be enlightened so that the interpretation that takes place in their hearts is based on the reality of who Jesus is and the glorious inheritance and power that he has passed on to them, rather than on their experience and expectations.

We need to claim this same prayer for ourselves. We need to ask God to enlighten our hearts with the truth of our glorious inheritance and the incomparable great power of Jesus that is there for us because we believe. We need our hearts enlightened with the authority we have through Jesus and, from this position of an 'enlightened heart', we are then able to create vision that isn't hindered by our assumptions or experience and is as big as Jesus would have us think.

I've had a deep lying assumption that I didn't really think about or know about until fairly recently. That assumption was that I was unlikely to see many miracles. I believed they happened but I didn't expect to see them personally. That assumption came because I didn't see many as I was growing up and most of the stories of miracles I heard about were from other countries. That assumption got blown out of the water when I was healed of partial paralysis!

Another deep lying assumption I've had is that God's work is in the church and therefore you can't expect the same level of supernatural intervention in workplaces. I've never consciously thought that, but it's been a background assumption that, looking back, has impacted on the way I've prayed for the work I've been involved in. Now I can see that assumption for what it is. I can also see how it impacted on me and what I need to do to move beyond it.

Thinking long

In my experience of supporting organisations with their strategic thinking, the planning is often undertaken as follows:
- we plan for a single future that is developed after we have done lots of data analysis and produced lots of trend analysis,
- we do that by extrapolating those trends into the future (that is, we use the past and present to create the future), And
- we don't often identify and question our assumptions about the future.

This is missing an awful lot! The future might not follow the same pattern as current events and the past. In our thinking and visions we need to think beyond linear progression and we need to think much longer.

Our vision needs to be about changing cities and nations in the long term, not the short term building of a particular church or business. The short term is still important, and needs a vision of sorts to achieve it, but it must be seen as a stepping-stone to the greater works that God is doing; not an end in itself. To do this we need God's perspective. We need to understand his heart and his plans. This only comes from knowing him.

My vision is to see the end of denominationalism and the restoration of the church as the beautiful Bride of Christ. I don't necessarily mean the end to denominations as I think it is great there are different expressions of church for different people. What I do want to see an end to is the mindset of competition that exists between churches. I long to see churches across the world that are united in the glory of Jesus so the world knows who God is. (Jn 17:23) I count this as thinking big!

When big, deep and long creates dissonance

When our visions are big, deep and long they can automatically create a dissonance, or inconsistency with our experiences and those we are leading. Their experience could be of only seeing one or two people become Christians each year, so a vision of seeing 1500 is so far from their experience that dissonance is created. It could be that their experience is of not seeing many healings, so a vision of creating a 'cancer free zone' or something similar, is so far from their reality that dissonance is created.

As part of our vision development we also need to create a right vision of the goodness of our Father. It is only when we begin to understand his nature, his goodness and his will for humankind that we are able to raise our expectations beyond our current experiences.

Sharing testimony is so important to doing that. When we share what God is doing we not only raise our expectations, but we are also inviting God to come in and do the same again. To create a vision that is big, deep and long we must first know how big, deep and long our Heavenly Father is.

Why is vision important?

The importance of vision is put very starkly in the Proverb; *'where there is no vision, the people perish'* (Prov 29:18 Amplified version). In some versions the word 'vision' is translated as 'revelation'. This shows that for us to lead our people in a way in which they thrive and live life to the fullest, our vision must be based on revelation from God. Our vision must come from knowing God's heart and his plans and strategies for our towns, cities, businesses and churches. When this kind of vision is present, as the Proverb goes on to tell us, the people are blessed. The word blessed could just as easily be translated as happy, fortunate or enviable. Vision is important because it keeps us going, it motivates us towards our goal as the travellers on the Oregon Trail found. Vision infused with revelation from God does this and more; it actually blesses us and others following it!

Vision also gives purpose and meaning. Paul, writing to the Philippians, said *'for me to live is Christ, but to die is gain'* (Phil 1:21). When he says gain he is talking about the gain of the glory of eternity with Jesus. His hope and vision for eternity gave him purpose and meaning whilst on earth. His vision motivated him to see the good news spread to the gentiles as far as he could take the message.

We need a God infused vision to develop real purpose and meaning in our lives and work. We need a vision to give us purpose and our staff and congregations need their own vision for them to develop real meaning and purpose in all areas of their life.

The journey that Holly and I are on at the moment is one of nailing down the vision that God has for us, but the mere fact of knowing we are going after a bigger vision that will involve doing what Jesus did whilst he was here on earth, gives purpose to what we are doing. With purpose comes that feeling of being alive, or doing what you were made to do. That feeling is right at the centre of living life in all its fullness.

Vision also gives direction and fulfilment.

Against all hope, Abraham in hope believed and so became the father of many nations, just as it had been said to him, "So shall your offspring be." Without weakening in his faith, he faced the fact that his body was as good as dead — since he was about a hundred years old — and that Sarah's womb was also dead. Yet he did not waver through unbelief regarding the promise of God, but was strengthened in his faith and gave glory to God, being fully persuaded that God had power to do what he had promised. This is why "it was credited to him as righteousness. (Rom 4:18-22)

Abraham and Sarah were far too old to have children, yet the promise God had spoken to them and the ensuing vision gave them direction and hope. Often when we use the word hope, we use it in the sense of an unlikely wish. That isn't the meaning here, the word 'confidence' or 'assurance' could quite easily replace hope and it would give the same meaning. Hope is the 'valve' through which faith operates. Hope is the bridge between promise and blessing. Hope, as expressed in a Godly imagination, fuelled and fed by the Word, allows faith to operate with more facility.

A key part of the vision of Abraham and Sarah is that it wasn't just for them. It was creating an inheritance for many generations to come. Their vision was from God and was certainly big, deep and long! It was big because their descendants would be more numerous than the stars in the sky. It was deep because the 'assumption' that they were past child bearing age didn't reduce their hope and it was long because it was for generations to come. In fact it was so long they wouldn't see the fulfilment of the vision in their lifetime. They were called to steward a vision that they wouldn't personally benefit from.

When we have vision we also possess joy, peace and hope in spite of hardship. Paul wrote to the church in Rome; *I consider that our present sufferings are not worth comparing with the glory that will be revealed in us.* (Rom 8:18) When we see the bigger picture the suffering is worthwhile because there is a purpose to it. The travellers on the Oregon Trail had a purpose that certainly gave them hope. When our hope is great it also gives us peace and joy during the suffering, it helps us to endure the sacrifice to make these visions become reality. We press on towards the prize because we know just how amazing the prize is and we have such hope and confidence that we will get it!

It is so common, in the church and in society more generally, for us not to understand the purpose of our trials and to let our circumstances rule us. We end up believing that everything is an obstacle that must be avoided. The second part of the Proverb mentioned earlier says; *"But happy is he who keeps the law"*. This use of the word law doesn't just mean the law given to Moses in the Old Testament, but is a much wider use to encompass our personal disciplines and boundaries that we develop to direct our lives through these obstacles. It is these obstacles that develop our character through which we become the people God needs us to be to step into the vision he has put in our hearts. That is why we, as Paul did, can take joy in the trials. We must view our obstacles as stepping-stones to conquer and walk over rather than barriers to avoid. It is through these obstacles that we learn more about ourselves and about God and position ourselves to step closer to the vision.

Developing vision

I use the following process when developing vision. Try it and see how it works for you:

1. Go to a quite place and make sure you have paper and a pen.
2. Remove any interruptions, particularly the phone, email and social media.
3. Ask God for inspiration and guidance. You want your vision aligned with His plan. Dream with him and don't be put off thinking 'is that my earthly desire'. You are a son or daughter and your Father listens to the desires of his children.
4. Write down your vision in detail. Write it in the present tense, as though it has already happened. This will make it more believable to you.
5. Test what you have written down. Is it big, deep and

long? What assumptions have led to it and did you discount anything you thought about before writing it down based on an assumption?

6. Share your vision with the people who have a stake in the outcome. Ask for their thoughts, insight and wisdom on it (Prov 15:22)

7. Commit to reading your vision daily. This is really important. "Faith is the evidence of things not seen" (Hebrews 11:1). The more you can "see" this, the more likely it will come to pass.

Leading others into their vision

To lead others into a full life you need to also give them permission to develop their own vision. Our traditional view of leadership is that the leader has the vision of where the organisation is going. A key role of the leader is to then communicate this vision so that everyone else buys into it and works towards it. The leader envisions the followers so together they effectively achieve the vision set out. I call that 'above the line leadership' and it can be described by the following diagram:

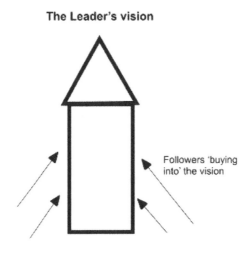

The Leader's vision

Followers 'buying into' the vision

This form of leadership is great for getting things done quickly and starting things. However, it creates followers, and thus by definition produces dependency. The level of 'buy in' to the vision is determined by factors such as: how good the vision is perceived to be, how well the leader is liked and trusted and whether the vision fits with the follower's view. If the buy in isn't good then the productivity won't be either.

This model of leadership reinforces the sacred / secular divide. The role of the majority of the congregation is to support the vision of the 'professional' Christian with finance and pre-determined action. The real work is done by the small number of 'professionals' and we pay them to do it. I am perhaps slightly exaggerating but you get the point. What if instead of creating followers we created leaders? What if instead of envisioning others to our vision, we released them into their own vision and together we retook our cites for God? The result is engaged and motivated people who are empowered as leaders. They have a purpose and autonomy to become masters in their area; all key factors in motivation.

The Leader's vision

This is a very different paradigm for most churches and businesses. Most churches have a leader who creates vision and 'volunteers' who follow the vision and turn it into reality. Most businesses have a leader who has a vision and the workforce is then employed to make that vision come about. There is nothing wrong with that model, but it doesn't get the best out of people and release them to be all that they can be. It in effect controls people towards a common goal. Releasing people into their own vision is risky and goes against common wisdom, but the rewards are enormous. More people will realise the extent of who God created them to be and will begin to live a full life as Jesus came to give.

The control we give away isn't to the people we lead. It is actually to God. Our vision is part of God's plan and so is the vision of the people we are releasing. Therefore if we release them to develop their own vision it will be in alignment with ours because both are in alignment with God's. Our role as leaders is co-ordination not control, but it can be a thin line between the two.

Google are a great example of this principle working in the corporate world. A few years ago Google gave all staff half a day to work on discretionary projects; the ideas they may have had and thought; "wouldn't it be nice if I had time to try that". This proved to be so successful that nowadays all employees at Google spend one to two days a week on these discretionary projects and the rest of their time on business as usual. It is through these discretionary projects that nearly all of Google's main products have been invented and developed. The whole company is more successful by helping staff to develop their own vision.

The staff at Google are given autonomy to get on with their ideas. They become masters in the area they are working on and derive a real purpose through the work. The result is motivated employees who are achieving great things for themselves and the company.

Ephesians 4 gives biblical agreement for this idea. In this passage Paul is describing the gifts of Jesus to the church namely: apostles, prophets, pastors, teachers and evangelists. Paul describes the role of these people to; *equip his people for works of service, so that the body of Christ may be built up until we all reach unity in the faith and in the knowledge of the Son of God and become mature, attaining to the whole measure of the fullness of Christ.* (Eph 4:12,13)

The whole point of these gifts to the church is to develop all believers into the people they were created to be. It is by developing the body of believers that unity is created and we reach maturity. Look what happens when we reach this maturity; we attain the whole measure of the fullness that Christ came to give us. The role of leaders in the church is to develop all believers so that they live in the fullness of Christ. We are not called to build bigger churches; we are called to build bigger people. Through this people are revived and pass this revival on.

It is also right for a leader to have a vision and sometimes to require service from others in the business or church after all Joseph was only released into his vision after first serving someone else's. The bible is very clear; we need to be servants as Jesus was. As a leader it is through the service of others that we see their character and are able to release them into greater things. However the focus should always be on the greater things with the service seen as a period of time, not their role.

Sometimes the vision of people is to serve the vision of another leader. That is excellent and many are called into this. However it is very different when someone discovers that their vision is to serve, compared to someone who doesn't even realise they could have their own vision.

This is summed up brilliantly by the following quote from AW Tozer in his book The Pursuit of God:

> *"Has it ever occurred to you that one hundred pianos all tuned to the same fork are automatically tuned to each other? They are of one accord by being tuned, not to each other, but to another*

standard to which each one must individually bow. So one hundred worshipers met together, each one looking away to Christ, are in heart nearer to each other than they could possibly be, were they to become 'unity' conscious and turn their eyes away from God to strive for closer fellowship."

When I was at University I met someone called Geoff who informally led me in the way I've just described. I first met him towards the end of my second year. He was a youth worker in a young offender's prison north of Newcastle and quickly I became involved in a lot of what he was doing.

Geoff was one of those people that you just said yes to without really knowing why, or realising what you had let yourself in for! I didn't spend nearly enough time studying in my final year as a result of getting to know Geoff, but I also did things I wouldn't have done otherwise. As a result I discovered things about my strengths, weaknesses and passions that I might not have otherwise come to know.

One of the things we did was to get a rap album recorded in the prison. I'd been running workshops in rap, DJing and breakdancing for the inmates who came to the bible study groups. We decided to record an album with their tracks and sell them to make money for the underprivileged children's charity, Barnardos, as many of the lads had been supported by the charity at some point in their lives. I persuaded another friend to bring his recording equipment to the prison and we created a studio in the prison chapel for a week. The inmates came and recorded their tracks before we got it mastered and produced.

I took on the role of marketing, something I'd never done before, and I loved it. We sold a few thousand copies of the album and got featured on many TV and radio stations and in various newspapers and magazines. I hadn't even considered marketing as a career before, but through this process I found something that I loved to do and which later on became my career. At no point did Geoff tell me what to do. He dreamt with me and together we created a vision for this project, and many others afterwards. We each had our own elements of the vision, but they came together to create something great. Through Geoff's leadership I was empowered to discover my own vision and passions.

Our role as leaders is to lead people to a realisation that God has a distinct vision and purpose for their lives. We must encourage them find this vision by helping them to think big, deep and long. We must inspire them to see with a Godly expectation, and we must not control by positioning them to serve our vision at the expense of their own. This requires us to trust God more as we are expecting him to align our vision with the vision of others'.

References

1. Festinger, L. (1957). *A Theory of Cognitive Dissonance*. California: Stanford University Press

2 Pink, D. (2009) Drive: the surprising truth about what motivates us: Riverhead

3. Let's Just Laugh at That, Steve Backlund, 2012.

5

Living purposefully – conquering our habits

We've looked at the need to have a purpose and instil a purpose in others. We've seen the importance of vision and the need to not only have our own vision, but also to empower those we lead to have their own vision. However, just having vision and purpose isn't enough. We also need to do something with it. Have you ever had a great vision, but deep down had a thought along the lines of: 'I know me, I know I can't achieve that' or even 'I've had big visions before but they never come off'?

To achieve the visions we have we need to move beyond 'knowing me' to 'knowing who God has made me to be'. It is a subtle difference but very important. To do this we must be purposeful in the way we think and act.

This chapter looks at creating a culture that is purposeful and focused on achieving what we want to achieve. It is different from the culture of purpose that the previous chapter looks at. That chapter is about having a purpose in your life; this one is about how to achieve that purpose.

The focus of this chapter is our habits. Our habits are powerful and have a large impact on us spiritually, emotionally and physically. We will look at identifying what our habits are and then creating strategies for breaking them and developing more purposeful behaviour.

The aim is to create a culture, individually for you as a leader, and within your organisations and families, that recognises the power of habits, identifies unhealthy habits, breaks unhealthy habits and replaces them with new, purposeful behaviours.

The impact of doing this is enormous. As you go through this chapter I encourage you to spend time reflecting, praying and putting new personal strategies in place. By taking control of our habits we move towards living a full life.

Our habits

Have you ever had the best intentions to start doing things differently? It could be many things; getting fit, managing your money better, investing more in relationships with children, spouses or work colleagues. It could be devoting more time to rest in God's presence, generally making better use of your time or focusing more on outcomes when planning. Whatever these intentions have been, how have you done at sticking to them? How often have your intentions smoothly and seamlessly become your normal way of doing things?

If you are anything like me you have struggled badly in this area. I could give you a list of the best intentions I have had that I haven't stuck at. Sometimes I have been incredibly passionate about the intention and yet I still haven't stuck at them. When I was younger sport was my thing, to begin with athletics and then rugby. I was pretty good and played at quite a high level, but the higher I played the more I realised that my natural talent, that had got me so far, wasn't enough to take me to the professional levels of the sport. There were many people with far more talent than me, so what I needed to do was put in the hard work, in fact harder work than the others to make up for the difference in talent. I really wanted to do this. I wanted to be a professional rugby player, but when push came to shove, I couldn't stick at this intention. My habit of training and working to an average level was stronger than my intention of working harder than everyone else. After a few weeks, I found I was doing what I had always done, despite the passion, the vision and the intention.

This phenomenon is not unusual. In fact it is very well researched. Psychologist Trandis led the way with his research looking at why people behave the way they do. He found three high level factors that influence our decisions; our habits, our intentions and the facilitating conditions. What's more interesting is that he found our habits are twice as strong as our intentions and the facilitating conditions put together[1] . So to put that another way; the frequency of what we have done in the past is the single biggest factor that will determine what we do in the future.

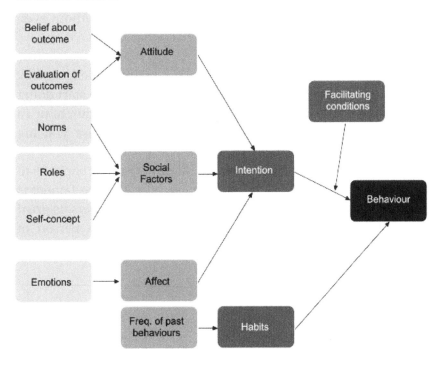

Think about this in terms of New Year's resolutions. You decide to get fit so you join the gym. You go religiously for the first week or so. Then you get a cold and miss a session. You have a busy day at work so you miss another. The kids are ill so you miss another and pretty soon you find that you are wasting the exorbitant gym membership you have signed up for and are tied into for another 11 months!

Cialdini, in his studies, identified how routine behaviour becomes detached from the original motivating factors; changing those factors (eg. attitudes or intentions) will not necessarily change the habit, as their power in influencing the behaviour has become weakened.[2]

Exactly this same phenomenon occurs in the workplace, in church and in our own spiritual life. Think about your workplace for a moment. Have you ever been on a training course where you've had a light bulb moment and you've thought; "Yes! That is exactly what I need to start doing to get the best out of my team." You go back to the day job with the best intentions to start doing whatever it was and without even realising it, you carry on doing exactly what you have always done.

What about in church; you've heard a really challenging talk at a conference, again you have the best intentions to start doing something, either in the way you are leading the church, or in your own spiritual life, and before long you realise you are doing what you have always done.

The good news is that we are not alone in this. It happens to us all and in fact, one of the real heroes of the New Testament is the archetypal example of this in his early life, but offers us great hope through the way he was transformed into a person of purpose.

Peter the Crumbling Rock

I love Peter. I think because there is so much about him in his early days that reminds me of me! He had great passion and intentions and moments of brilliance, but that was combined with pride, fear and failure!

If you look at Peter, pre the resurrection, he is a great example of a 'good Christian', in fact, by our standards, a 'really good Christian'. He gave up his job to follow Jesus and spend time with him. He dedicated three years of his life to becoming a disciple of Jesus. He sat at his feet and was taught by the master, not only through what Jesus said, but also by experiencing first hand his nature, the behind the scenes Jesus that we don't read about in the gospels. He saw Jesus conduct amazing miracles; from the feeding of the 5000, walking on water, healing large numbers of people and freeing large numbers from demonic oppression. He took part in many of the miracles himself; the feeding of the 5000 only happened when the disciples took the five loaves and two fishes and went out in faith amongst the crowd. He was commissioned by Jesus to go out and conduct miracles himself, and he did. He even walked on water, albeit for a short period!

Peter was also present at what must have been a quite astonishing event. He was there at the transfiguration (Mt 17:1-13). Imagine you were there with Peter. Jesus invites you to come up the mountain with him and when you get to the top, the glory of heaven comes upon Jesus and his face starts to shine like the sun and his clothes turn brilliant white. Now I'm sure you've looked at the sun before, it is so bright it actually hurts your eyes and can do them damage. That's the brilliance with which Jesus was shining! It wasn't just something to look at though. His face was shining with the glory of heaven. To be in the presence of that glory must have been an immensely powerful event that would have impacted Peter, James and John greatly.

If the transfiguration had just stopped there it would have been quite some event, but then Elijah and Moses also showed up on the mountain. Now remember these disciples were Jews and Elijah and Moses were all time Jewish heroes. It would have been like the most famous historical figures that you had grown up learning about in great detail, suddenly being there in front of you, still with Jesus shining like the sun!

It didn't stop there either! Next, to add to this smorgasbord of an experience, was the audible voice of God. God's voice boomed out (I'm using artistic licence with this, we don't know how loud it was) *"This is my Son, whom I love; with him I am well pleased. Listen to him!"* (Mt 17:5). If the disciples had any doubts as to whom Jesus was and his veracity, it would have been blown away at this point. In fact this whole experience must have been transformational.

So here we have Peter. A passionate man who is desperate to serve Jesus and to be the best person he can be for Jesus. We know this from when Peter asked, "Who is the greatest" (Lk 9:46). He really wanted to be the best that he could be. Even if his motives weren't completely right at that point, the passion was right, the passion to be all he could be for Jesus. Peter also had a clue as to what his destiny might be, what 'being the best' might mean for him. When Jesus first called him to lay down his net and follow him, he changed his name from Simon to Peter (Jn 1:42) because Peter means the rock, and Jesus told him he would be the rock that the church would be built on.

Now if someone came along and told me to change my name and called me something different it would be pretty significant for me. I'd remember it; I'd want to know more about why and what the plans were. When would I be used to build the church? I'm sure it was the same for Peter. Any prophetic act from someone credible would stick in my mind, but coming from Jesus, the son of God, well that would really be memorable. I bet this was some of the thinking behind his 'who is the greatest' comment. He was the one who had had this prophetic word from Jesus. He was the one whose identity had been changed so significantly and symbolically right from the beginning in readiness for something that was coming in the future. He knew that his destiny was great.

So Peter had passion to be all he could be and had some idea as to what this meant. He had received teaching, intensely for three years, from Jesus himself. He had seen Jesus perform miracles and had performed miracles himself. He had had one of the most significant spiritual experiences that possibly any person has ever had. Yet at the hour of Jesus' greatest need, Peter betrayed him. He denied him three times (Mk 14: 66-72), despite being warned by Jesus he would and being prepared for it.

Peter had the best intentions, but despite the best training programme known to man that included; teaching for the mind, practical action and spiritual experience; Peter still reverted to Simon. His habits of being Simon, of not being extraordinary, of not living in the fullness, were stronger than his intentions and his training.

The good news is that this isn't the end for Peter. Jesus didn't call Peter into his destiny when he first met him and then leave him to see if he could conquer himself and qualify for the destiny that he was called into. Exactly the same is true for us too. When we first meet Jesus he invites us into a destiny. He invites us to live in the fullness of life here on earth and to go on a journey where his plans and purposes for us are slowly revealed. He doesn't just leave us to do this in our own strength and see if we sink or swim.

Peter did become the rock the church was built on, the destiny that Jesus called him into when he first met him. If you read the bible from Acts onwards there aren't any accounts of the old Peter, Simon, if you will, resurfacing and failing despite his best intentions. So what happened? How did Peter become the rock?

Transformation of Mind

When writing his letter to the Romans, Paul wrote:
"Do not conform to the pattern of this world, but be transformed by the renewing of your mind. Then you will be able to test and approve what God's will is – his good pleasing and perfect will" (Rm 12:2)

Sounds good doesn't it, that we can be transformed by our minds being renewed. Our minds are central to our habits and in fact all of our behaviours, something we will explore more in the chapter on Influences. Therefore this is a key for us breaking our habitual behaviours, habitual ways of thinking and of being revived. Having our minds transformed is key for us to live in the destiny that each of us were called into when we first encountered Jesus and of living life to the fullest.

There are two aspects to this renewal of mind and both aspects have implications to living in the fullness of Christ and leading those in our churches and workplaces into that fullness. The first of these aspects is allowing the Holy Spirit to work in power and transform us; the second is creating the environment and the invitation for that to happen through the development of our spiritual disciplines.

Dramatic renewal through the power of the Holy Spirit

The word used in the Greek to describe the transformation of mind in Romans 12 is the same word that is used to describe the change that happened to Jesus at the transfiguration. Remember that, when the glory of heaven rested on Jesus so his face shone like the sun and his clothes became bright white. Now that sounds like some transformation!

So this passage in Romans isn't just telling us we should have a renewed mind by making an effort to not conform to the patterns of the world, but is in fact showing us how the power of the Holy Spirit can have this amazing, radical transformation. The same power that made Jesus' face shine like the sun, is available to transform our minds, our thoughts and therefore our behaviours and actions.

I've seen this in action, in a dramatic one off event and in a less immediately dramatic, but nonetheless fundamental way over a longer period.

The dramatic event happened for my wife Holly. In February 2013 some crazy American evangelists came to town. Or we thought they were crazy then and they certainly were in comparison to normal church life in Norwich, UK where we live. We were in the middle of our journey of drawing closer to God and looking for theology that explained the healing I had experienced the year before, so we decided to go along to the revival meetings that Charlie Shamp and Munday Martin were running.

The style of the meetings was quite different to our past experiences, but we knew the Holy Spirit was there and we were expectant for God to show up and work in us all. At one point in the meeting they prayed for 'transformation of minds'. Holly described a feeling of her head burning and then freezing and then burning again. A great experience, but actually Holly's mind really was transformed!

Holly often felt frustrated that the bible didn't seem to come alive for her as it does for other people. However, from that moment on it has become so alive that it's like she walking through 3D bible pages. As she reads the bible now, she gets large amounts of revelation as to what the passage means and how it links to other parts of the bible. This didn't happen for her before this prayer, she has received no training in the meantime and suddenly, through a prayer for the 'renewing of her mind', she now reads the bible in a whole new way and hears God speak to her through it.

I've never had such a dramatic experience. However over the last two years my mind has also been renewed to a similar point, but through more of a gradual journey than a one off hit. This renewing of our minds is central to the personal revival we are experiencing at the moment and the full life that we are living.

Creating the environment for renewal of mind

The bible gives clues of a process that we go through for the renewal of minds and the breaking of habits that stop us living in the fullness. Now a process is there as a guide. It isn't to say that this is the only way that God works and that if we don't follow all of these steps we won't be set free from these habits. However, I do believe it is useful to be able to see how they link up, and for visual learners like me, a diagram can say a 1000 words.

The first stage has to be to identify what habits are holding us back. Some of these might be obvious, but others will be hidden and you may not even be aware of the effect they are having on your life and the way they are stopping you from living life to the full.

Ask the Holy Spirit to show you what these habits are. It could be they are habits in the way you are thinking and lead you into believing a lie about the way God sees you. We will tackle this more specifically in the chapter on Self Expectations.

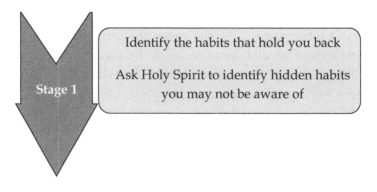

Stage 1

Identify the habits that hold you back

Ask Holy Spirit to identify hidden habits you may not be aware of

The bible talks about the concept of co-labouring (1 Cor 3:9). We do some of the work and God does some of the work. The transformation of mind is a case in point. God certainly has the power to act sovereignly and transform someone's mind as he did with Paul on the road to Damascus. Or at least create such an 'event' that someone can't help but want their mind to be transformed. However I think the more normal way that this happens is through co-labouring; we do some of the work to create the environment for a transformed mind and the Holy Spirit does the rest.

A particular 'habit' that Holly and I suffered from until a few years ago, was a habitual way of being critical, seeing the worst in people and looking for the negative. I don't know how this crept up on us as this wasn't the way I had been raised, but we found ourselves in this position. Whatever we were involved with, we managed to 'critique' the other people involved to see the bad side of them and of course, a better way that we would have done it!

We realised we were doing this and wanted to change, but by this point in time it had become a strong habitual way of thinking. We didn't really want to do 'it' and we felt 'dirty' afterwards, but we also found a perverse, short term satisfaction from putting others down behind the quite of our own front door. Changing this mind set and habitual way of thinking has largely followed the process I'm outlining.

Bracing our minds

In Peter's first letter he wrote; *'Therefore, prepare your minds for action; be self-controlled; set your hope fully on the grace to be given you when Jesus Christ is revealed'* (1 Pet 1:13).

In the Amplified translation is says:

So brace up your minds; be sober (circumspect, morally alert); set your hope wholly and unchangeably on the grace (divine favour) that is coming to you when Jesus Christ (the Messiah) is revealed.

Both of these translations suggest action and effort that we have to take. We have to prepare our minds or 'brace up our minds'.

This concept of 'bracing our minds' is central to a lot of the academic studies that look at how to stop acting habitually. The premise is that we fall back into our old habits, our old behaviours, usually sub-consciously without even realising we are doing it.

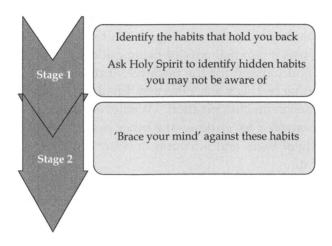

'Bracing our mind' acts to increase the power of our intentions so that our habits don't win the war on our behaviour so easily. Remember the work by Trandis written about earlier in the chapter? His findings resulted in the following equation:

$$Habits = 2 \ X \ (intentions + facilitating \ conditions)$$

Well if we can strengthen our intentions so we remain conscious of them more often, then we begin to redress this equation.

In the corporate world of executive coaching 'don't do lists' are becoming really popular. Some of you may be the organised type of person who writes 'to do' lists, well this is the opposite. The idea is to write down the habits that you are trying to stop and to put that list somewhere visible where you will see it frequently throughout the day. It works particularly well if the list is placed near to where the habit is undertaken, that is if there is a particular geographical location for the habit you are trying to stop. By making your intentions more visible, you increase awareness of what you are trying to do and reduce the chance of subconsciously falling back into the habit.

Using the example of our negative attitude towards other people; the need to change was very apparent and the desire, the intentions, was also increased as the Holy Spirit gently convicted us of it to such a point that the perverse satisfaction that we used to feel disappeared and it was only a 'dirty' feeling that was left.

Refocusing your mind on hope

Also important is what we prepare our minds with and for. In the passage in 1 Peter it says to prepare our minds by setting our hope wholly and unchangeably on the grace, or divine favour, that is revealed through Jesus. So we brace ourselves by focusing on the hope we find in Jesus. Thoughts of fear, worry, anxiety, selfish ambition, vain conceit are not allowed to enter into our thinking because of our focus on a greater hope. We have to fight against them and rebuke and banish these thoughts when they enter our heads. We do this by bracing our minds to the hope we have in Jesus. A brace literally connects you to the thing you are bracing yourself to. We have to connect ourselves so strongly to the hope we have in Jesus and the divine favour we have from him that other thoughts cannot pull us away from this place. Part of our hope will be the vision and purpose we have as we explored in the previous chapter.

In the letter to Colossians, Pauls writes *let the Word of Christ dwell in you richly* (Col 3:16). Looking again at Peter and his transformation of mind, we see the combination of a dramatic renewal of mind through the power of the Holy Spirit at Pentecost and the bracing of his mind by focusing on the hope Jesus has given the disciples.

Jesus had promised them the Holy Spirit and had told them

not to leave Jerusalem until they had received the gift of the Holy Spirit. They knew the gift was coming and they knew how good it would be as Jesus had taught extensively on it, including telling them they will do even greater things than him when they received the Holy Spirit. Jesus then told them to wait in Jerusalem after he had ascended back to heaven until they received this gift. Well I reckon, despite sadness at Jesus going again, they would have been excited and expectant. They waited together in the upper room praying. If I imagine myself there, I can imagine a battle to 'brace my mind'. On the one hand they would have braced their minds and focused on the hope Jesus had given of the Holy Spirit coming, his grace and divine favour and of some of the plans and purposes that Jesus had commissioned them to fulfil. On the other hand there would have been many forces trying to tear them away from the brace. Fear, anxiety, feeling lost without Jesus, being unsure about exactly what the plans were, possibly feelings of unworthiness linked to past failures. By focusing on Jesus' promise and the hope found in that, they were dwelling with the Word of Christ that he had given them.

The Holy Spirit then turned up at Pentecost, Peter and the other disciples were transformed, the church was born and the gospel began to be taken to all nations.

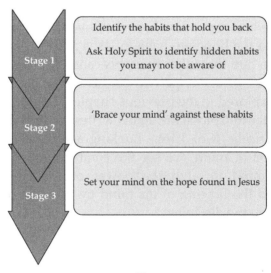

In organisations it is important to focus attention on the positive results you will get by behaving differently. This is the premise behind DEEP. It provides facts and figures to show leaders the impact on productivity if they change the way they lead. The hope they gain further strengthens their intentions to behave differently and to stick at these new behaviours; bracing themselves to this hope despite many other forces encouraging them to revert to their old ways.

Part of breaking a stronghold is to act in the opposite spirit of what you trying to stop. I remember reading a book when I was younger about the Argentinian revival. I can't remember who the author was or the title of the book, but there is one particular section that I have always remembered. A mission team was in Cordoba, the fashion capital of Argentina. They weren't getting the breakthrough that they had in other places and while praying about it, they discerned that it was because a spirit of pride had a stronghold over the city. The whole mission team then knelt down in the main square of the city to cry out in prayer. The physical act of kneeling down in prayer in public, is the exact opposite of pride. They were undignified! This physical act in the opposite spirit broke the stronghold and the revival began in Cordoba.

The same is true for our personal strongholds. We sometimes need to consciously act in the opposite spirit. Holly and I began to do this to try and crack our negative attitude by consciously seeing the good and talking about the good in other people.

Finally, brothers and sisters, whatever is true, whatever is noble, whatever is right, whatever is pure, whatever is lovely, whatever is admirable – if anything is excellent or praiseworthy – think about such thing (Phil 4:8)

Expectation

Focusing on hope and dwelling in the Word are important in changing habits. Another ingredient is to change the mind-sets we have that limit our behaviour. Focusing on hope and the Word takes our minds beyond the limits of everyday natural life, to the supernatural plans, purposes and promises of God. We need to free our minds to think beyond our experience and not to limit our theology to our experiences.

Making assumptions about what is possible and can be expected is a natural thing to do. We need to 'brace our mind' consciously against this so we can hope with Jesus' eyes, which are without limit.

I came across a fascinating example of this recently:

> *The Iron Curtain was traced by an electrified barbed-wire fence that isolated the communist world from the West. Deer still balk at crossing the border with Germany even though the physical fence came down a quarter century ago, new studies show.*
>
> *Czechoslovakia, where the communists took power in 1948, had three parallel electrified fences, patrolled by heavily armed guards. Nearly 500 people were killed when they attempted to escape communism.*
>
> *Deer were also victims of the barrier. A seven-year study in the Czech Republic's Sumava National Park showed that the original Iron Curtain line still deters one species, red deer, from crossing.*
>
> *"It was fascinating to realize for the first time that anything like that is possible," said Pavel Sustr, a biologist who led the Czech project. Scientists conducting research on German territory reached similar conclusions.*
>
> *The average life expectancy for deer is 15 years and none living now would have encountered the barrier.*[3]

The deer alive today have never experienced the electric shock that their ancestors would have done. Yet they still don't cross the border where the fence used to be. They have become so conditioned by their expectations and the expectations passed down to them they can't hope for anything more or anything different.

The same can happen to us. We become so conditioned to our environment, experiences and teaching that we often don't hope for anything more or anything different. We don't even realise that more is possible or available.

Dwelling on the Word, on the promises made, on the reality of who Jesus is, on our identity as sons and daughters and the authority we have been given through Christ, is vital to transforming our thinking and our minds. Through this we can break free from habits that hold us back and move forward to live in the fullness that Jesus came to give us.

This brings us back to vision. The vision must lift people's eyes up beyond the everyday to something aspirational. It needs to help people see what could be possible. It needs to excite and tantalise people at the possibilities if the vision is realised. This is the same for churches and businesses. For a church, the vision could be for the multitudes of unbelievers that could become part of the body. For the business, it could be about growth, customer service or something else. The key is that the vision takes people beyond current performance and experience and gives them a glimpse of what is possible.

Our words are powerful in creating and sustaining the hope that is needed. In Joel 3 it says *'Let the weak say I am strong'* (Joel 3:10). The Hebrew is simply Gebor 'ani, "Strong I", with the verb to be understood. This certainly means 'I am strong', but it also means at the same time 'I will be strong', and even 'I have begun to be strong'. So it is both an affirmation of faith and a promise for the future. So we must proclaim we are strong even when we are not, because the truth of who Jesus has created us to be is far more important than our current circumstances. We know the promise for the future, that we will be strong.

When the angel of the Lord appeared to Gideon he addressed him as 'mighty warrior' (Judges 6:12). Gideon was anything but a mighty warrior at that point in time. He was a weak and cowardly farm hand. The angel of the Lord addressed him as the person he had been created to be because that was more important than his current circumstances. In doing so, he called into existence that which was not (Rom 4:17).

The same applies for us personally and for our organisations. We must declare that we are living in the fullness and our effectiveness is not compromised by our habits. We must also declare and prophecy over our organisations that they are living in the fullness. By doing so, we also call into existence that which isn't yet.

The word 'dwell' is also important to consider. In Hebrew there are two words for 'dwell' that have quite different meanings; yashav, which is an individual dwelling and shakan which means dwelling in a community. The word used in the Colossians passage we looked at earlier; 'let the word of Christ dwell in you richly', is linked to shakan. This means that letting the Word dwell in us isn't just about meditating on the bible, but about being in a living community, a real relationship with The Word, who is Jesus.

It is also important to dwell on the truth in our churches and businesses, although perhaps this looks slightly different. It is about dwelling on what is possible, not on where you currently are. Looking at what others are achieving, finding 'best practice' and looking at the best out there raises our horizons to what is possible. We need to expect more than we are currently doing so we don't become the Red Deer and limit ourselves by our experiences and our predecessor's experiences.

In this process we also need to ask the Holy Spirit to show us what is possible. Sometimes we have become so conditioned by the environment we are in we find it very difficult to see anything different. Ask the Holy Spirit to show you what is possible and raise your horizons.

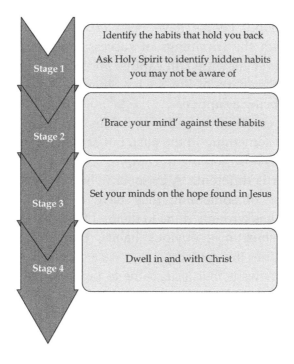

Captives and Prisoners

In Isaiah 61 Jesus outlines his purpose. He said he came for the poor, broken hearted, captives and prisoners. We also know that Jesus came for all of mankind, so it is possible to conclude that all of us fit into one of these four categories, or at least have in the past.

The words 'captive' and 'prisoner' are interesting. It is easy to think of them as being the same thing, but looking at the passage, Jesus came to do different things for the two groups. He came to 'proclaim freedom for the captives' and to 'release from darkness the prisoners'. The root of the two words also shows a difference. The root of the word 'captive' is linked to being captivated. This perhaps suggests people have been taken captive by first being captivated by something.

This is so true in the corporate world, particular higher up the organisation. People have been taken captive by being captivated with the trimmings of success; money, power and status. However they are still captive and not living life to the full. Often other parts of life, such as marriage and family can suffer due to being a captive.

The same can be true with our habits. We may have been captivated by something in the past, but actually it isn't healthy and the habit is now holding us captive.

A prisoner is different. A prisoner is held against their will either because of something they have done, or something someone else has wrongly done to them. I think that some more serious and sometimes obvious habits, that are particularly unhealthy, fit into this category.

The good news is that Jesus came to proclaim freedom from captivity and release from darkness for the prisoners, so even if we fit into these two categories, the result is the same – freedom!

How do we sustain it?

Having our minds transformed and tackling habitual behaviours and patterns of thinking, is not a one off event. In the letter to the Ephesians Paul wrote: *And be constantly renewed in the spirit of your mind [having a fresh mental and spiritual attitude]* (Eph 4:23 Amplified version). We need to be constantly renewed. We need to constantly invite the Holy Spirit to renew our minds and to consciously 'brace our minds' against the patterns of behaviour and thinking that we are trying to avoid.

The result of this is personal revival. The result is living life to the full as Jesus promised. In his writings to the Romans Paul said; *'but those who live in accordance with the Spirit have their minds set on what the Spirit desires. The mind of a sinful man is death, but the mind controlled by the Spirit is life and peace'* (Rom 8:5,6).

The mind controlled by the Spirit is life and peace. When our minds are transformed and we allow the Spirit to control our minds constantly, not just for a one off spiritual experience, then the result is life. The result is living in the purposes and plans Jesus has for us and called us into when we first met him. The understanding that these plans are perfect, that they are the absolute best for us, also gives us peace as we no longer rely on our own understanding, but are transformed in the knowledge of the greater truth that Jesus is.

In essence this brings us freedom. 2 Corinthians 3:17 says; *'Now the Lord is the Spirit, and where the Spirit of the Lord is, there is freedom'*. So when we dwell on His word and allow the Spirit to control our minds, consciously bracing ourselves against others ways of thinking, then actually we are freed from the habits that hold us back, both the behavioural ones and patterns of thinking. This links back to the Isaiah 61 passage. What are the habits that have either held you captive or taken you prisoner? Inviting the Spirit of the Lord to control your mind frees you from them.

Renouncing the habits, repenting from them and inviting the Spirit in to purposefully come and take control of your mind, puts authority back where it should be. You take authority over the habits and you pass that authority over to the Lord.

The role of other people

As Trandis' equation has shown us there are two factors that can help to outweigh the power of our habits. They are our intentions and the facilitating conditions. We've already looked at increasing the power of our intentions by 'bracing our minds' as described in 1 Peter. The other aspect to look at is increasing the power of the facilitating conditions.

It would be very plausible to argue that the power of the Holy Spirit completely changes this equation and perhaps is the change in the facilitating condition that immediately and comprehensively throws this whole equation out of the window. This is certainly true in some cases, however, in others, I believe

God uses the principle of co-labouring to develop us and maintain our free will.

This is what James describes when he says; '*Consider it pure joy, my brothers and sisters, whenever you face trials of many kinds, because you know that the testing of your faith produces perseverance. Let perseverance finish its work so that you may be mature and complete, not lacking anything*' (James 1:2-4).

By co-labouring with God we develop. We have our faith tested which produces perseverance and perseverance develops maturity. Maturity meaning that we aren't lacking anything we need to live life to the fullness.

If this is right, then there are probably things we can do as part of our co-labouring to increase the effect of the facilitating conditions. The bible offers various ideas and instructions that fit into this category. The most stark and obvious one is when Jesus said; "*If your right eye causes you to stumble, gouge it out and throw it away. It is better for you to lose one part of your body than for your whole body to be thrown into hell. And if your right hand causes you to stumble, cut it off and throw it away. It is better for you to lose one part of your body than for your whole body to go into hell*" (Mt 5:29,30).

If you are aware that something is causing you to continually revert back to unhealthy habits that are holding you captive or prisoner then get rid of that something!

Sometimes it isn't that easy or obvious. The bible is clear that we aren't designed to live our life and to run the race in isolation. Living in an open, transparent and accountable relationship with other people improves the 'facilitating conditions'. In doing so the equation is redressed and so is the power of our habits.

James tells us to; '*confess your sins to each other and pray for each other so that you may be healed*' (Jam 5:16). The word translated as sin in this passage, hamartia, suggests more of a weakness or a tendency than an actual act. Having loving relationships where we are open and accountable for our weaknesses, tendencies and what we are doing, especially the things that we don't want to be, has real power. When this is combined with the transparency about the new behaviours that we are trying to put in their place, it can be transformational. Notice the passage doesn't tell us to confess our sins to God, but to each other. There is a release and power in removing what is hidden and bringing it into the open. We have also been given all authority in heaven and earth and therefore, Christ in us, the confidence of glory means that we actually have power. We have the power of Jesus, through the Holy Spirit to break the chains that are binding people when following unhealthy habits, if they confess those habits.

The second part of this verse; 'so that you may be healed' shows the result of this. When we confess our sins to other people, the secret shame no longer has a hold on us and Christ in us restores us.

This same idea is referred to in Colossians. Paul tells the believers to; *'Let the message of Christ dwell among you richly as you teach and admonish one another with all wisdom through psalms, hymns, and songs from the Spirit, singing to God with gratitude in your hearts'* (Col 3:16).

We are told to 'admonish one another'. This means holding each other to account and to do that properly we need to give other people permission to hold us to account. In fact the meaning is much more than our view of holding someone to account. The Greek verb used is noutheteo, nous means 'mind' and tithemi means 'to set', so noutheteo means 'to set in someone's mind'. The New Testament word for mind actually meant something much more than just the mental processes that go on in our head between the ears. The mind was almost another way of describing the soul, so the word admonish did not just mean wagging a finger at someone and saying "you could do better". It meant saying things that are going to affect someone at a very deep level in their soul.

A lot of the successes people have had in changing culture in organisations at a corporate level have been in creating 'peer accountability networks' within the workplace. This is a great example of awful management speak, but the essence that underpins it is good.

When trying to introduce new behaviours, or break old habits, making people more aware is very important. If a whole group of people are supporting each other in making this change, then this drastically improves the strength of the 'facilitating conditions'.

Peer accountability networks are just groups of people who have all given permission to hold each other to account when they spot other group members behaving in a way they are trying to change. In fact they are often even more proactive than that, they regularly ask people how they are doing at ...., whatever it might be.

When this works best it isn't heavy or judgemental. It is a group of people, often in a very light-hearted way, reminding each other of what they are trying to do and what the result will be if they manage it. It can be a bit 'sticky' at first because we are such private people and live such a long way from the close church community we see described in Acts. However I find it works. It makes people realise they are not in it alone and that together, they can crack it, whatever 'it' is. It brings the secret personal battles into the open so that the community supports each person to achieve their goals. It transforms the 'facilitating conditions' and topples the scales on Trandis' equation. After all, we are the body of Christ and bodies are amazing at healing and 'correcting' themselves.

Creating a purposeful culture in your organisation

Habits are important and getting a grip on them is vital to living life in the fullness. It is important that we do this personally as leaders, but it still leaves the question; how do I create a culture within my organisation that gets a grip on habits so that individually and corporately we are living in the fullness?

The following are my ideas for doing this and they apply to both churches and businesses:

1.) Ask the Holy Spirit to identify habitual strongholds in the organisation – You are the light on a hill in your organisation and Christ is in you. The first step is to pray for your organisation and expect God to reveal to you strongholds that the Kingdom of Heaven can break into. Prayer should obviously be a constant through the rest of the stages identified below as well!

2.) Involve colleagues from across the organisation to also identify habits, both in terms of behaviour and thinking, which limit what is possible in the organisation.

3.) Get an understanding of what could be possible if these habits weren't there and were replaced with positive ones. When possible combine facts, figures and numbers with stories. This is where 'best practice' and case studies from other organisations similar to yours can be useful. Another useful starting point is to reflect on times when the organisation has worked really well and delivered above expectations. What are the characteristics of this time? What did it feel like for those involved? From these points of success imagine what it would be like if these were the norm. What would it be like if the high points that you have experienced were the everyday way of working. What would you achieve and what would it be like for each individual involved.

4.) Create a strong and compelling vision through this process. This should be done through involvement with as many people as possible. The aim of the vision is twofold; to create dissatisfaction personally and corporately with the current state and to show what the future will look like. It is important to consider fear and loss in this process (see chapter on fear and loss).

5.) Strengthen hope by continually sharing stories of how you are moving towards the vision. Over time it becomes normal and expected that you are heading towards the vision. Over time the vision becomes more realistic and achievable in people's minds. This increases motivation to play their part in achieving it.

6.) Create the environment for the culture change by equipping each individual to 'increase their intentions' and as groups strengthen the 'facilitating conditions'. This is done by helping each individual personalise the corporate culture change down to their individual habits and behaviours and then creating peer accountability networks so that people support and encourage each other to stick with the new behaviours.

7.) Ensure staff 'dwell' in the vision. Consistently and constantly communicate the vision and the associated new behaviours. In direct marketing there are three key words that are used to ensure campaigns are effective. They are; recency, frequency and potency. If a prospect has seen your message recently, they are far more likely to take action. If they hear the message frequently, they are also more likely to take action and if the message is potent to them it again increases the chances they will take action. The same applies to the leader's communication during this period. The chance that people buy into the vision and into the habitual changes that are necessary is increased if hearing about it is recent, frequent and potent. Potency is created through a very personal approach to leadership. When the leader works with staff to create peer accountability networks, when they are visible and their efforts to changes are transparent, then the message is more authentic and potent. This is dealt with more in the chapter on the personal characteristics of leaders.

References

1. Trandis, H 1977. *Interpersonal Behaviour.* Monterey, CA: Brooks/Cole

2. Cited in Maio, G, B Verplanken, A Manstead, W Stroebe, C Abraham, P Sheeran and M Conner 2007. Social Psychological Factors in Lifestyle Change and Their Relevance to Policy. *Journal of Social Issues and Policy Review,* 1 (1) 99-137.

3.http://www.huffingtonpost.com/2014/04/23/deer-iron curtain_n_5200163.html

6

Creating Culture Not Conforming

Early on in my career I worked for a company that wasn't a happy place. It was going through a large change and there was a lot of internal politics and jostling for power. The result of this was a culture of negativity that spread like a cancer. Groups of staff couldn't have a normal conversation without talking about certain key issues. Everyone had an opinion, these opinions differed but the result was negativity, pessimism and ultimately depression.

I enjoyed work, was very ambitious and consciously decided to distance myself from these unhealthy dynamics. However, without realizing, it affected me badly. I never really joined in the negative talk, but the environment sapped the life out of me, took any joy out of the work and made me look for a quick exit! The culture of the workplace had affected me. It had influenced my outlook on life and was robbing me of my chance to live life to the full.

At about the same time Holly and I were living in a unique community in rural Norfolk. It was a converted Victorian workhouse that now consisted of 37 houses and flats. It was located outside the main village in its own grounds and was really very isolated with fields as far as the eye could see in all directions. When we arrived, there was a degree of community life and spirit, but with the normal neighbourly disputes thrown in for good measure. Our house was situated next to one of the communal garden areas and, largely due to Holly's sociable nature; it quickly became a hub for 'community bonding'.

Over the time we were there this community became incredibly strong and shared most things. Most evenings in the summer different groups of neighbours would have a BBQ or drinks and there were regular parties. The community really became family.

It wasn't all down to us, but Holly particularly was the catalyst. The way she acted in this community became a model that influenced others and as a result, a family emerged. We moved house after living there for seven years as our family grew. We hated moving, but just couldn't fit into the house any more. It was such a wrench but we visit frequently and have many close friends there still.

These two stories demonstrate how we are influenced by culture and by others. One story demonstrates how I was influenced very negatively and the other shows how we, as a family, helped to have a positive influence to change a whole community.

The fact is we are influenced by other people. Realising this is important to understanding why we make the decisions we do and behave the way we behave. More important however, is learning how to control the impact influences have on us and how to develop a culture within our organisations that develops and nurtures through generating positive influences. When we do this we start the journey of personal revival and move towards living life in all its fullness.

This chapter explores how we are influenced, what we can do about it and how we can turn round cultures so they become positive influences. It will also look at what to do if you are stuck in the middle of a negative or possibly evil culture.

The aim, as throughout the rest of this book, is to find the key to living life in all its fullness for us individually and for the people we lead.

What influences us?

We are influenced by others on a variety of levels. The highest level is the culture that exists in the communities we are part of. As culture changes it influences us. One example of this is the way elders in society are viewed and how this has changed over time. I'm not using this example to make a point about honouring our elders, although it could easily be used to do that, but merely to look at how changes in culture influence us and our behaviours.

When my parents were children they addressed other adults as 'Sir' or 'Madam'. When I was a child I addressed other adults as 'Mr Smith' or 'Mrs Jones'. My children address other adults by their Christian names, as do the vast majority of other children. The expectation society has on the way adults are addressed over these three generations has changed and the last three generations of my family has adapted to this change. My family has been influenced by culture changing and followed suit.

At a different level we are influenced by patterns and trends in culture. Fashion and hairstyles are good examples of this. When I was a teenager, a centre parting, long curtains and an undercut were all the style. I followed this style and have many embarrassing photos to remind me! Looking around today I can't see any young people with a haircut like that, probably just as well!

Also during my teenage years, with my curtains and undercut, my Dad bought a white Ford Sierra with a spoiler on the back. I thought it was the best car going and loved arriving to school or to friends' houses in it. Fast forward a few years and white became such an unpopular colour for a car that if you were buying a second hand car and had a choice between a white one and pretty much any other colour, the white one would have been considerably less expensive because the colour was so unpopular. Nowadays white cars are en vogue again and represent a large percentage of new car sales. As these trends and patterns change over time, we are influenced by them and follow suit.

The third level of culture we are influenced by is the culture of the groups that we belong to. This includes the organisations and the extended families we are part of. If you think about your family and compare it to other families you know, I'm sure you can pick out some pretty large cultural differences. This becomes particularly obvious when it comes to marriage and then is highlighted further when the first baby comes along and the cultures of parenting you were used to suddenly become so important even though you vowed as a child to never do the same to your kids!

We are influenced by culture. To live life to the full we need to dig a bit deeper to understand how and why it influences us in the way that it does. Psychologists Tajfel and Turner demonstrated that we find our social identity from the groups that we are part of[1]. They found we strongly favour people in the groups that we are in, even if those groups don't represent anything and people have just been randomly assigned to them. So just being part of a group, whether or not we like the others in the group, agree with what it stands for, or do anything in the group, creates an allegiance to it. This means that the groups we are part of, both formal and informal have a strong influencing affect over us. This form of influence is vital for our churches to understand as the 'tribalism' that this influence creates can be very positive and also damaging. On the positive side it creates strong community and family within the church but it is also a major factor behind the disunity in the church. It is easy to lose sight of the wider body of Christ because of our strong allegiance to the particular church, or group, we are part of. We won't look too deeply at the impact of this form of influence, but recognising its power on us and on the organisations we lead is vital to living revived lives in the fullness of everything Jesus has for us.

The fourth level of cultural influence is the people you spend the most time with. Psychologist, Albert Bandura, showed that people learn by observing what others do.[2] He found that we copy the behaviours of others. If the behaviour is good and positive then this can be a positive trait. If it is negative behaviour then the impact on us is also negative.

Cialdini built on this research to show that we actually look to others to see how to behave, especially in; ambiguous situations that we haven't encountered before and in crisis and when we perceive others to be experts.[3] In his original experiment he had some accomplices stare upwards on a street pavement as if they were looking at something although there was actually nothing there! Other people quickly joined them and a large group formed and stayed there long after the accomplices actually left.

I'm sure you've experienced going to an event for the first time and you consciously look at how other people are behaving and, what they are doing becomes your guide for the way you should behave. A friend of mine recently went to an event organised by a Christian ministry. He arrived a bit late and sat at the back. He comes from a very charismatic / Pentecostal church background and is used to interacting with speakers during their talk with comments such as; 'preach it', or 'hallelujah'. He had been to this venue many times and knew the ministry it was run by was from a similar culture to him. He started to interact with the speaker in the same way as normal and quickly found many heads turn round and glare at him! They had come from other churches with a very different culture and his behaviour was so foreign to them and was also foreign to the culture that had already been set at the event. If he had been there from the beginning then maybe that would have set the culture differently.

All of these influences; culture, group and individual could influence us for good, for bad or it could be neutral. The point is that they do influence us and it is important to understand how and why so we can control the impact.

Reflect on the different forms of influences I've mentioned so far:

- The groups you are in
- Experts
- When we are in crisis
- When in ambiguous situations
- People we like
- People with power over us
- Culture at societal levels, organisations level and extended family level

How do these different areas and groups influence you? How positive or negative are the influences?

Mind, heart, strength and soul.

Imagine that something happens to you, let's keep it simple for the moment and say that 'the something' is a friend at church ignores you and doesn't talk to you. This event will affect your emotions and make you feel a certain way. This in turn will impact on your behaviour and actions.

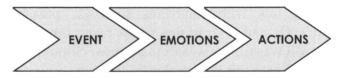

However the process isn't actually as simple as this. There is a stage missing. An event occurring doesn't just impact on our emotions. It impacts on our emotions based on our interpretation of the event. Our mind is critical to the way we react to situations.

Let me give you an example: imagine you are at a Christian

conference and you really want to talk to the main speaker. You have read all of their books, love everything they say and, if you are honest with yourself, have fallen into the Christian celebrity following trap! Anyway, you are at this conference and it's a lunch break and you see the main speaker near you speaking to someone else. You decide to pluck up the courage to go and speak to them so you 'hover' near them waiting for him to finish their conversation. You know what it's like, you feel uncomfortable and awkward so you try and look natural and busy, perhaps busily checking your phone for that important message or looking across the room pretending you are trying to see someone else and you aren't really waiting next to the speaker ready to pounce!

You are standing just to the right of the speaker and they finish their conversation. They seem to look right past you, don't notice you, look to their left, see someone else and start talking to them.

This is 'the event', you were waiting to talk to the speaker, they don't notice you and they talk to someone else.

You could interpret this event a number of ways and it is this interpretation that will result in different emotions. You could interpret it as follows:

"I don't believe it. He doesn't want to speak with me. He saw me but just didn't want to speak with me. I don't blame him really, not many people want to speak with me. In fact no-one does really. There isn't much about me that would make people want to speak with me. I'm completely uninteresting, struggle for conversation, I always seem to bore people and man I'm so ugly he probably saw me out of the side of his head and decided to steer clear."

This interpretation of the event would lead to emotions of depression, lack of self-worth and possibly worse!

These emotions would in turn lead to a specific set of behaviours, most likely withdrawal, sitting by yourself and losing any motivation to speak with anyone.

Exactly the same event could be interpreted completely differently:

"Would you believe it? I was standing on his right and he looked to the left and saw someone he knew. What are the chances of that!

This would lead to a different set of emotions; possibly increased determination and motivation to be more obvious so he doesn't 'slip through the net' next time. In turn the behaviours and actions could even involve doing star jumps right in front of the speaker so you definitely won't be overlooked next time. It could ultimately lead to a restraining order, but that's another issue!

So it isn't the event itself that impacts on our emotions and actions, but the combination of the event and the way we interpret it in our mind.

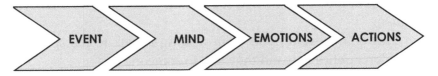

EVENT   MIND   EMOTIONS   ACTIONS

It is the same when looking at the way people and culture influence us. The people and the culture themselves aren't the only factors that lead to changes in our emotions and behaviour, but the combination of the people, culture and our interpretation. This means, to really understand how to get to grips with the way we are influenced personally and to ensure influences within our organisations are positive, we need to look at both what is influencing us and our reaction and interpretation of it.

So what is influencing us and how important is it? I think it is useful to dig into the process I've described a bit more. When Jesus was asked which the greatest commandment is, he replied; *"Love the Lord your God with all your heart, with all your soul, with all you mind and with all your strength. (Mk 12:30)*

Jesus didn't do things accidentally. So he wasn't just reinforcing the point by showing four different ways to love God. Each one of these ways is actually separate and shows us more about how to love God and how he loves us.

Loving the Lord God with 'all of our mind' is not just about our intellect, but is more about our thoughts and in fact our whole patterns of thinking. Loving with all of our heart is about loving him with our emotions. Loving with all of our strength is about loving him with our actions and loving with all of our soul is about loving him with everything we have got. The Greek word translated here as 'soul' is translated as 'life' in other parts of the New Testament, so this is an all-encompassing one – love him with everything.

So let's look at this list of how to love God:

It's remarkably similar to the process we looked at earlier. Our mind, and what we feed it with, is central to not only being able to love with all of our mind, but also our ability to love with all of our heart, strength and soul. It is only when we control our mind and purposefully love with all of it, that we are able to control our emotions and then love with all of our heart. When this happens we can then control our actions and love with all of our strength. Therefore, getting to grips with what we feed our minds with, our influences and the way we let it influence us, not only has an impact on living life to the fullness, but also our ability to keep the commandment Jesus said was the most important!

In fact the root of all of the 10 commandments is our mind. Jealousy, anger and lust all directly lead to specific actions that are in the 10 commandments. Therefore the way we control our minds determines our ability to keep any of these commandments. Each of the emotions involved with the areas targeted by the 10 commandments, would have resulted from some external event or influence, so the combination of influence and mind is central to keeping the commandments.

So what are the influences we are feeding our minds with; using the language of the process described earlier – what is 'the event'?

The Event

The book of Psalms starts as follows:

> *Blessed is the one*
> *who does not walk in step with the wicked*
> *or stand in the way that sinners take*
> *or sit in the company of mockers,*
> *² but whose delight is in the law of the Lord,*
> *and who meditates on his law day and night.*
> *³ That person is like a tree planted by streams of water,*
> *which yields its fruit in season*
> *and whose leaf does not wither –*
> *whatever they do prospers.*
> *⁴ Not so the wicked!*
> *They are like chaff*
> *that the wind blows away* (Ps 1:1-4)

The passage starts by talking about what our influences are and what we need to do about them. It says that blessed is the person who doesn't step with the wicked or stand in the way that sinners take. By saying that you are blessed if you don't do things, it is also saying, by default, that if you do these things you won't be blessed.

The next section of the Psalm says that you also won't be blessed if you sit in the company of mockers. Mockers is a word we don't use often, but it is talking about people who talk badly of others and of God. They make fun of them, maybe to their face, maybe behind their backs. Maybe even in a very 'holy' way 'helpfully' pointing out others' bad points to members of the church! Doing this forfeits us from the blessing as much as being wicked. In fact just associating with people doing this also disqualifies us. Disqualification by association, that's pretty harsh, but it shows how seriously God takes this.

Why are we disqualified if we just associate ourselves with these people? It's not that God disqualifies us, but we disqualify ourselves. The influence of these people will affect us. What they do will feed into our minds, which in turn feeds into our emotions, which in turn feeds into our actions. We become polluted by the influence of these people.

It's true, think about a time you've spent with a really negative person. I'm sure you find it pretty easy to think of one. The best that happens is that you come away feeling drained and wiped out, often far worse happens, you find yourself joining in the negativity.

When we allow these influences into our minds, hearts and actions, then we are forfeiting ourselves from the blessing the Psalm talks about because we are not keeping the two greatest commandments. We are not loving God with ALL of our mind, heart, strength and soul and we're not loving our neighbours either.

Have a look at verse two: 'but whose delight is in the law of the Lord, and who meditates on his law day and night'. This shows us how to get the blessing. To get the blessing we have to take positive action and control what influences we allow into our minds. We have control over how much of the most powerful form of influence we allow into our minds, the presence of God. When we delight in the Lord and meditate on him day and night we allow him to be the influence that infuses our mind, impacts on our emotions and changes our behaviours. He changes our motivation by showing us heaven's perspective on events, not our interpretation. Jesus is the law, he made the old law redundant and replaced it with his love, so when we meditate on his love, on the person of Jesus and allow Jesus to be 'the event' that we feed our minds with, we receive the blessing, we don't disqualify ourselves from it.

In other parts in the Psalms it talks more about what happens when we make the presence of God 'The Event' that we feed our minds with and allow to be the major influence on us. Psalm 84 says:

Blessed (happy, fortunate, to be envied) are those who dwell in Your house and Your presence (Ps 84:4 Amplified Bible)

When we dwell in the presence of God we are blessed, happy and fortunate.

Psalm 23 reads:

Surely only goodness, mercy, and unfailing love shall follow me all the days of my life, and through the length of my days the house of the Lord [and His presence] shall be my dwelling place (Ps 23:6)

When we dwell in His presence; goodness, mercy and unfailing love will follow us all of our life.

Psalm 16 declares:

You will show me the path of life; in Your presence is fullness of joy, at Your right hand there are pleasures forevermore (Ps 16:11)

In the presence of God is joy forever more.

These three verses from the psalms tell us that when we dwell in the presence of God we are blessed, happy and fortunate. Goodness, mercy and unfailing love will be with us for all of our life and we will also have joy for all of our life. Wow. Doesn't this sound just like the picture of fullness I spoke about in chapter 2? If we control the influences we allow into our minds and make the presence of God the overriding influence, we are revived, we live in the fullness of life that Jesus came to bring us.

Verse 3 of Psalm 1 says; *'That person is like a tree planted by streams of water, which yields its fruit in season and whose leaf does not wither – whatever they do prospers'.*

This picture of trees planted by streams of living water is a recurring picture in the bible. You can find the same picture in Ezekiel 47 and Revelation 22. Have a look at Revelation 22 below:

Then the angel showed me the river of the water of life, as clear as crystal, flowing from the throne of God and of the Lamb down the middle of the great street of the city. On each side of the river stood the tree of life, bearing twelve crops of fruit, yielding its fruit every month. And the leaves of the tree are for the healing of the nations.

The passage describes a city which has the throne of God in it and from which a river flows that has the tree of life on each bank.

This is a picture of restoration for us individually and for the church. Once restored, no evil can enter the city (Rev 22:15) and it is a stronghold of the good and righteous. This links to Jerusalem in Solomon's time when there was no 'adversary' in the city. (1 Kings 5:4)

God is saying to us that he will create strongholds of his presence where he sits on the throne where the river of life flows from. There are two keys to setting up these strongholds:

1. Holiness, purity and a humble and contrite heart. – (Rev22:14) *'Blessed are those who wash their robes, that they may have the right to the tree of life and may go through the gates into the city'.* This washing of robes is a deep cleaning that will deal with hidden 'dirt' we might not even be aware of.

2. Hunger, or more accurately, thirst for what God has for us – (Rev22:17) *'whoever is thirsty, let him come'* this is quoting what Jesus said in John 4:13 'Jesus answered, *'Everyone who drinks this water will be thirsty again, but whoever drinks the water I give them will never thirst. Indeed, the water I give them will become in them a spring of water welling up to eternal life'.*

Jesus said this during the festival of Tabernacles which is a time of praise and thanksgiving for God's goodness and provision.

When we 'wash our robes' or allow Jesus to wash our robes by revealing deep and hidden influences that are clinging onto us, then we 'have the right to the tree of life' (Rev22:14). The leaves of the tree of life are for the healing of the nations (v2). So when we remove bad influences; spiritual ones as well as natural ones, and allow the presence of God to be our source of influence, then our fulfilled life overflows and impacts others, it heals the nations, it heals our businesses, churches, communities and families.

What we see is what we will be

There are other passages in the New Testament that talk about us changing to become like the influences we allow in. This can be incredibly positive if the influences are positive and particularly if the influence is Jesus. In his second letter to the Corinthians Paul wrote:

And we all, who with unveiled faces contemplate the Lord's glory, are being transformed into his image with ever-increasing glory, which comes from the Lord, who is the Spirit (2 Cor 3:18)

So when we contemplate the Lord's glory, when we think about it, dwell on it and allow it to enter into us, then we are transformed into this same image. The glory of the Lord that we allow to influence us is then what we become. *Christ in us the hope of glory* (Col 1:27), or in other translations, the 'confidence' of glory. When we spend time in the presence of God, we are transformed into his likeness.

The letter to the Colossians continues in this theme: *'Do not lie to each other, since you have taken off your old self with its practices and have put on the new self, which is being renewed in knowledge in the image of its Creator'* (Col 3:9,10)

When we put on our new self that we find in Jesus, we are renewed in the image of the creator, we become more like Jesus.

So if we are renewed in the image of the creator, it is important that we have the right image of the creator or else we will be renewed into a counterfeit image that doesn't reflect who he is. The chapter on leadership characteristics looks at this in more depth.

How is culture influencing us?

So the influences we are under, through the people we spend the most time with and the cultures we are in, impact on us and change us. This can be positive or negative but understanding it is important to living life in all its fullness.

It is normally easier to think about the way individual people influence us; looking at how culture impacts on us can be much trickier as it is more subtle and can tap into such deep held beliefs that we don't realise there is another way of thinking or acting.

Take the example of Joan of Arc. French culture had two deeply held assumptions at that time that completely influenced governmental decision making and life in general for the vast majority of French people. They were; that the English could never be beaten and that women could never do anything meaningful.

These paradigms of thinking were so deep that it wasn't talked about, it was just accepted and thoughts and actions came from a place of acceptance rather than questioning and challenging to see if it is true and if there is a different way to think.

It took a maverick, who was ultimately killed for being so radical, to challenge the paradigm and change the culture of France. It was because of Joan of Arc that the French finally realised the English could be beaten and eventually foreign and military policy changed and as a result the French gained freedom.

All organisations and groups have such paradigms; the unwritten and, often not thought about, assumptions that influence us and guide the way we act.

A common assumption in some churches has been that miracles no longer happen, or at least not in the Western church.

This has changed actions and ultimately theology resulting in healing not being prayed for and people living without the power of the Holy Spirit.

What deeply held assumptions influence you? Reflect on this and ask the Holy Spirit to reveal any hidden assumptions you are not even aware of.

To really understand what forms and reinforces the culture of your organisations, and therefore what is influencing us, it is necessary to look a bit deeper. A useful model for doing this is the Cultural Web.[4] This helps to identify what is creating and reinforcing the assumptions or paradigm that sit at the heart of the culture you are in. It facilitates the breaking down of the culture into six different aspects.

The six aspects are:

Stories – not the formal communiques, but the informal stories that members of the group or organisation talk about in private.
- What core beliefs do stories reflect?
- How persuasive are these beliefs (through levels)?
- Do stories relate to:
  o   Strengths or weaknesses?
  o   Success or failure?
  o   Conformity or mavericks?
- Who are the heroes and villains?
- What norms do the mavericks deviate from?
- Do they include testimonies of God's goodness?

Routines and rituals of members of the group
- Which routines are emphasised?
- Which would look odd if changed?
- What behaviour do routines encourage?
- What are the key rituals?
- What core beliefs do they reflect?
- What do training programmes emphasise?
- How easy are rituals/routines to change?

Organisational structures of the group
- How mechanistic/organic are the structures?

- How flat/hierarchical are the structures?
- How formal/informal are the structures?
- Do structures encourage collaboration or competition?
- What types of power structure do they support?

Control systems of the group
- What is most closely monitored/controlled?
- Is emphasis on reward or punishment?
- Are controls related to history or current strategies?
- Are there many/few controls?

Power structures of the group
- What are the core beliefs of the leadership?
- How strongly held are these beliefs (idealists or pragmatists)?
- How is power distributed in the organisation?
- Where are the main blockages to change?

Symbols of the group
- What language and jargon are used?
- How internal or accessible are they?
- What aspects of strategy are highlighted in publicity?
- What status symbols are there?
- Are there particular symbols which denote the organisation?

This model applies to all organisations we are part of, the churches we are in and the groups and friends that we associate ourselves with. Below is a simplified cultural web analysis for two different churches. Both of these churches are charismatic and evangelical and would pretty much agree in the main theological areas. However look at how different the cultures are:

	Church 1	Church 2
Stories	The church growing larger, supporting smaller churches and taking over and revitalising struggling churches	God moving in power in signs wonders and miracles through members of the congregation
Symbols	Large building, multiple services,	Band on a stage, Separate prayer house Name badges for staff and students
Power	Employed team and those with the time to volunteer the most	Church leaders, those seeing God move miraculously and those who have 'served the longest'
Organisational Structures	Main leader and employed core team together with some power for a few members of the council '	Hierarchical; staff and cascading to the students
Control	Few controls as long as there is a clear fir with the vision	Strong principles of serving and developing relationship
Routines and Rituals	Multiple services, Children involved Some liturgy that only priests can do	Time in prayer house, many services

The culture that exists in these churches impacts on the congregation for good and for bad. It impacts on the way they make decisions, what they view as important and ultimately how they see themselves in relation to their Father.

Have a go at creating your own cultural webs for the groups you are part of, the church you are in and your workplace. Break the culture down to identify what is creating and reinforcing it. What are the influences that are not only forming the culture, but are also influencing you? What can you do about them?

The following two stories show how small changes in the stories that are told in an organisation, can change the culture and the underpinning paradigm.

These stories are based on two real examples; the first a large multinational business. The new CEO recognised there was a negative culture pervading the organisation and realised success depended upon doing something about it. He realised that the 'stories' that were told in the organisation were largely negative and that a 'glass half empty' philosophy dominated the business. He decided to change this by introducing a new approach that he started informally by modelling it himself before initiating it as company policy. He did this by simply starting every meeting with a good news story of something good that had happened in the company in the last week.

As good news became a more spoken about topic, he found that over about six months it eroded the power of the negative culture that existed. People began to think of 'what had gone well' ready for the next meeting they had to go to. The act of thinking differently, of allowing positive stories to influence them, made them change their outlook and actually be more positive.

The same is true in churches. Bill Johnson, at Bethel, a church in Redding California, started a similar routine; of sharing a testimony of what God had done before every meeting started. This raised expectation, increased faith and invited God to 'do it again' as the word testimony comes from the Hebrew word for 'do again'.

The culture we are in influences us, so we have a responsibility to ensure the culture that is influencing us is as positive as possible. As leaders we have the responsibility to change the culture of our organisations so that it is positive for the people who are working for us or are part of our congregations. By doing so, the organisation will also achieve its purpose far more effectively and individuals will be revived and start to live life to the fullness.

What happens when we are in a bad culture?

This all sounds great. However sometimes we are in a culture that we can't do anything about, certainly not in the short term. Some organisations I have worked with, particularly when they have been through a major change process, have a really negative culture. Depression, anger and despair are so rife you could cut it with a knife.

If you are in a culture like that, you may not be in a position to change it and you may not be in a position to remove yourself from it as you need the job to pay your bills. You may also feel called to be part of it so you can be salt and light and change it from the inside out.

If this is the case, what can you do so the culture doesn't change you? In a sense, most of what I've written in this chapter so far suggests that culture will influence us whether we like it or not. However this doesn't have to be the case. Culture, and those we spend the most time with, do influence us, but through good strategies, personal discipline and the grace of God enabling you to be who you've been called to be and to do what he's called you to do, despite the culture; it is possible. Daniel is a great example of this.

Daniel was captured in Jerusalem and taken to Babylon in 604 BC. He then served various different Babylonian Kings for around the next 70 years. Daniel wasn't just in a foreign culture; he was in a culture that actively tried to stop the Jews practising their faith and killed many for it. Daniel didn't give into the culture and he didn't go into hiding, he flourished and changed it from the inside out.

The culture Daniel was placed into when he was taken captive as a boy was hostile. He was a foreigner in a culture so alien to him and so against much of what he stood for. Does that sound at all similar to pressures you can feel when working in secular organisations?

Think about some of the pressures he was under in relation to the eight cultures of engagement or fullness that this book is based around:

- **Meaning / Purpose** – Living under foreign rule and not being allowed to publicly serve his God would have drained purpose and meaning from Daniel. Seeing Jerusalem destroyed and God's people taken captive could well have caused Daniel to question God and doubt his promises.
- **Habits** – he was being forced into new habits that were not only different, but went against his religion. Jews were called to live apart from the world and here was

Daniel being forced to very much be part of it.

- **Influences** – many unhealthy and evil influences were central to the Babylonian culture. Once Daniel gained a place in the higher courts of society he would have been exposed to these influences even more
- **Personal Leadership Characteristics** – His leader had just ransacked Daniel's homeland and there are many examples throughout the lives of the different kings Daniel served, of brutality and cruelty
- **Self-Expectations** – It would have been easy for Daniel to doubt himself, although there is no record of this happening
- **Loss** – Daniel saw Jerusalem destroyed and God's people taken captive
- **Working to strengths** – Daniel quickly found he was very good at all the Babylonians asked him to do
- **Involvement** – Daniel had no power, to begin with, to influence his own destiny

So Daniel was in a foreign land, with a foreign religion that was hostile. He was metaphorically in the lion's den already. The elements of engagement that need to be in place for us to live a 'revived' and full life were largely not there. Yet Daniel prospered! How did he do this?

There are several central aspects of Daniel's story that we can take as principles to apply to our lives when we are in foreign and hostile cultures:

Daniel co-laboured with God – the principle of co-labouring is a theme that runs through each of the chapters in this book. We do some of the work and God does some of the work. We see this early on in Daniel's story when he decided to take a stand and not to eat the food of the King, but instead eat vegetables.

But Daniel resolved not to defile himself with the royal food and wine, and he asked permission not to defile himself in this way. Now

God had caused the official to show favour and sympathy to Daniel. (Dan 1: 8,9)

Daniel took the first step by being brave and asking permission not to eat their food. Once Daniel had done his bit, then God also joined in the work and 'caused the official to show favour and sympathy to Daniel'. When we step out in faith and do our part, God does the rest through supernatural power. When we take a risk and put our faith in God he is always there for us.

The trap that Daniel could have fallen into, and we often do, is worrying about what people would think of him. For Daniel this worry would have been particularly understandable because the consequences could quite literally have been death.

For us, when in difficult cultures, it is very easy to fall into the trap of thinking; 'if I do this, or make a stand on that, will they think I'm weird and make my life even worse and what chance have I got of being relevant and sharing the gospel then'.

I don't know if you've ever added in the 'holy justification'? What chance will I have of sharing the gospel then? It is easy to justify these decisions and when we do it enough, we might even believe them! The truth is, if we ask God, he will let us know when to make a stand and when not to. The Holy Spirit will prompt you, but you might need to practice hearing from him and recognising the language he speaks to you in.

Daniel honoured the authority he was under - Daniel lived as a captive, serving a King that had ransacked his homeland. However Daniel didn't actively oppose the regime. He didn't even do it as a subversive who had gained trust in high places so he could bring the regime down at a later date. He was able to influence policy decisions through the position he gained, but it seems that this wasn't his primary agenda.

Throughout the story of Daniel he honours authority. We see this right from the beginning when he asked permission from the chief official not to eat their food. When Daniel was given a task to do, he did it to the best of his ability and excelled in it. He studied hard and became the best of the best to the extent the King found none equal to Daniel, Hananiah, Mishael and Azariah. (Dan 1:19) Later in Daniel's life we read that he *'so distinguished himself among the administrators and the satraps by his exceptional qualities that the King planned to set him over the whole kingdom.* (Dan 6:3)

When plotters against Daniel tricked the King into passing a decree that would stop Daniel from worshipping God, he didn't complain. Daniel didn't stand by the water cooler and influence others to rise up against this unfair and discriminatory practice. Daniel quietly went to his room and honoured the higher authority, God, but not in a way that publicly dishonoured the King. (Dan 6:8-25)

The bible is clear that all rulers, good and bad, are appointed by God. In the letter to the Romans Paul writes; *'Everyone must submit himself to the governing authority, for there is no authority except that which God has established'.* (Rom 13:1)

He then carries on and says; *'Therefore it is necessary to submit to the authorities, not only because of possible punishment but also because of conscience. This is why you pay taxes, for the authorities are God's servants, who give their full time to governing'.* (Rom 13:5,6)

Jesus also confirmed that all authority is appointed by God. Just before he was crucified and Pilot was questioning him they had this conversation:

"Do you refuse to speak to me?" Pilate said. "Don't you realise I have power either to free you or crucify you?"

Jesus answered, "You would have no power over me if it were not given to you from above. Therefore the one who handed me over to you is guilty of a greater sin". (Jn 19: 10,11)

So if all authority is appointed by God, it is right that we honour authority, in fact it is our duty. This means if we don't agree with them or we think they are making a bad decision or, in fact, if we think they are doing evil things, we can't stop honouring them. Daniel honoured the authority he was under, and God and man blessed him as a result.

In Paul's letter to the Colossians we are told; *'and whatever you do, whether in word or deed, do it in the name of the Lord Jesus, giving thanks to God the Father through him'*. (Col 3:17)

Daniel set us the example of honouring authority in the way he interacted with those with power over him, the way he interacted with others outside the gaze of authority and in the way he also worked his hardest and did his best.

We are called to do the same. We are called to always honour those in authority over us, to honour them in front of others, not incite rebellion and to work our hardest for them as part of our worship.

Daniel was humble – Daniel did some astonishing things when in the service of the King, particularly in the field of dream interpretation. However, whatever Daniel did, he didn't take the glory himself, but always praised God for it. (Dan 1:17, 2:19) I think an even great testament to the humility of Daniel is the way he didn't expect anything, or rather, he didn't feel he was owed anything.

When things went against him, which they did in spectacular fashion, he didn't complain, he didn't incite a rebellion; he got on with it and put his trust in God.

This bears a remarkable similarity to the picture of humility that is written about in Philippians 2. In this passage we hear about Christ's humility and are told to copy it:

5 In your relationships with one another, have the same mindset as Christ Jesus:

6 Who, being in very nature God, did not consider equality with God something to be used to his own advantage;7 rather, he made himself nothing by taking the very nature of a servant, being made in human likeness 8 And being found in appearance as a man, he humbled himself by becoming obedient to death – even death on a cross!

9 Therefore God exalted him to the highest place and gave him the name that is above every name,10 that at the name of Jesus every knee should bow, in heaven and on earth and under the earth,11 and every tongue acknowledge that Jesus Christ is

Lord, to the glory of God the Father.
[12] Therefore, my dear friends, as you have always obeyed – not only in my presence, but now much more in my absence – continue to work out your salvation with fear and trembling, [13] for it is God who works in you to will and to act in order to fulfil his good purpose.
[14] Do everything without grumbling or arguing, [15] so that you may become blameless and pure, "children of God without fault in a warped and crooked generation." Then you will shine among them like stars in the sky [16] as you hold firmly to the word of life. And then I will be able to boast on the day of Christ that I did not run or labour in vain. [17] But even if I am being poured out like a drink offering on the sacrifice and service coming from your faith, I am glad and rejoice with all of you. [18] So you too should be glad and rejoice with me.

Jesus made himself nothing and became the lowest of the low, despite the fact that he actually did deserve to be placed at the most distinguished place at the table. We are told to also act in this way, to expect nothing without grumbling and complaining. This is completely counter cultural. Society teaches us that we have rights. We deserve to be treated a certain way, and when we aren't, we are within our rights to complain about it and tell others. I think this is one of the hidden assumptions, or paradigms, that can influence our thinking without us realising. Jesus didn't give this model, the letter to the Philippians tells us the exact opposite and the life of Daniel demonstrates what happens when we become humble like Jesus was.

When we get it right this passage tells us we will; *'shine like stars in the sky and hold firmly to the word of life'.* (Phil 2:15,16) That is exactly what happened to Daniel. He was humble, he didn't expect anything, he realised he had no earthly rights and focused on the heavenly reward. When we forfeit our earthly rights we gain our heavenly rewards.

He not only became a 'star' in the Babylonian society, but also held firmly to the word of life. This is a promise! When we humble ourselves as Christ did we hold onto the Word of life; we live life to the fullness as Christ promised, we are revived, we have purpose, we step into our destiny.

Daniel relied on hearing from God to make hard decisions – One of the hardest things to do is to know when to make a stand, especially in the light of what I have just said about honouring authority. Daniel made some really interesting stands: he made a stand about what to eat, but not about what they called him. They changed his name to Belteshazzar which means 'prince or protector of Bel' in place of Daniel which means 'God is my judge', and he didn't make a stand about this!

Daniel committed himself to pleasing God and heard from God to help him direct his decisions and know when to make a stand.

We need to do the same; we need to quieten our minds to allow us to hear the Holy Spirit's promptings. We need his inspiration to know when to make a stand. We need this inspiration particularly when it seems to be a grey area and the difference between these promptings of the Holy Spirit and our deep routed assumptions or paradigms that infuse the way we look at life, is not clear.

So to summarise; to survive and in fact thrive in a hostile culture that seems to drain us of life we need to:

- Co-labour with God, we work hard but ask and expect God to also work supernaturally
- Honour the authority we are under even if they seem wrong and evil. We do this by working our hardest, doing everything asked of us to the best of our abilities and not dishonouring them through talk with others
- Humble ourselves by laying down expectations and rights just as Jesus did
- Be in constant communion with the Holy Spirit to know when to make a stand and when not to

So we are influenced by others, by the culture we are in and the people we spend the most time with. Spend some time understanding the influences that you are under, particularly the deeply help assumptions.

Once you've identified them it's time to do something about them. Which influences are positive and how can you increase the influence they have in your life? Which ones are negative? Can you remove them? If you can't remove them then follow Daniels example and thrive in the culture and change it from the inside.

If there are negative influences you can't remove, you can make them less important by placing the presence of God as the principle influence in your life. This will revive you and you will begin to live in the fullness of life as Jesus intended us to do.

You also need to lead others into a place where negative influences are cut off and their primary influence is God and his goodness. Have you ever wondered why God wants us to worship him? Yes he is worthy, but why does he need us to tell him? Doesn't it sound a bit egotistical? He wants us to worship him because he knows that we become like whatever we worship. Therefore, if we worship him and he is our primary influence then we actually also become more like him. That is why our primary calling as humans is to love the Lord God with all of our heart, soul, mind and strength.

References

1 Tajfel H and Turner , J (1986) The Social Identity theory of inter-group behaviour' in S. Worchel and L.W. Austin (eds) *Psychology of Intergroup Relations* (Chicago, Nelson-Hall)

2 Bandura A (1977) *Social Learning Theory* Englewood Cliffs, NJ: Prentice Hall.

3 Cialdini R (1993) *Influence: Science and Practice* (3rd edn), New York, Harper Collins.

4 Johnson and Scholes (2002) *Exploring Corporate Strategy*, Prentice Hall, London

7

Self-Expectations – identity and authority

We need to have a vision, a purpose for what we are doing. We need to co labour with God and act purposefully so we see that vision come to life. We also need to understand the way we are influenced by the cultures we are in and the people we spend time with. With this in place we can continue with our purposeful pursuit of our vision and to lead others into their vision.

The next piece of the jigsaw is to view the present and the future in the way God does. We must expect him to act as the mighty and loving God that he is and we must expect him to use us. Do you *really* believe you can achieve the vision you have by co labouring with God? Do you have nagging doubts that 'things like this don't happen to me'? When you read Psalm 37:4: *'Take delight in the Lord, and he will give you the desires of your heart'*, do you think that your desires will be given to you or do you internalise all sorts of logical and theological reasons as to why this doesn't apply to you and your dreams and visions? Do you rationalise the lowering of your expectations?

Having right expectations is so important to achieving our vision. The bible is clear about this, just read Hebrews 11, a whole chapter about heroes of the bible who had the right expectations because of their faith. Secular studies also prove this to be true; people who achieve are usually those who expect to achieve. So what do healthy expectations look like? How do we develop them and how can we lead others in a way so they also have healthy expectations of themselves and of what God will do through them?

There are a number of different facets to developing healthy expectations. In Christian / church language it is to do with our understanding of our identity, our authority and the goodness of God. In workplace / psychological language it is to do with our self-efficacy and our self-discrepancy. When both are put in the context of what scripture says about who we are in God, they actually look very similar!

For us to know what it means to live in the fullness of life and be revived, it is absolutely essential to know who we are, who God is and who we are in God. Without knowing who we are and who we have been created to be, then there is no chance of living in the fullness as we won't know what is possible. If we don't know God, then we have no idea as to the fullness of his plans and purposes for us. We limit ourselves by thinking of what is possible in our terms, not God's.

Identity

Higgins' self-discrepancy theory[1] suggests that at any one point in time we have three views of ourself: who we think we are, who we think we should be and who we think other people think we are. When there is a disconnect between these different views it is likely that we start becoming hard on ourselves, negative self-talk begins and ultimately we become depressed and lose engagement and motivation.

The way we think of ourselves and perceive what others think of us, can be a mine field if we don't understand our identity as sons and daughters of God.

- If our view of 'who we are' is warped then it is likely to create a disconnect between 'who we think we are' and 'who we think we should be'.
- If our view of 'who we think we should be' is warped then it is likely to also create this same disconnect
- If our view of what others think about us is warped or even that we worry about this when we shouldn't, then it will create a disconnect between 'who we think we are' and 'who we think other people think we are'.

It is really important that we, as leaders, are secure in our identity and model a healthy internal dialogue that flows from this security. The culture we live in is actively fighting against us having a right and balanced view of who we are, who we should be and what others think of us. Culture teaches us to worry about what others think of us, to put on a front and, to some extent, actively try and create a disconnect between these three areas of our thoughts because; 'what people think is more important than the reality'. We need to model a healthy identity to those in our churches and workforces because, in so doing, we release them to also know their identity.

Who do we think we are?

In a few church services I've used an illustration from Mike Bickle's book 'After God's Own Heart'[2]. I've asked the congregation what they think God's overwhelming emotions are towards them. Do they think he is largely mad, sad or glad? Mad at how much they let him down despite what he has done for them. Sad because they let him down and don't have the relationship he wants them to have or glad; he rejoices over them no matter what.

A small majority of people, in my very unscientific survey, have gone for the sad option with a roughly even split between glad and mad for the remainder.

This is quite telling. The majority of believers think that they are still rotten sinners who continually let Jesus down and disappoint him. In the workplace the same thought patterns exist but without the biblical references for them. People remember their failures and are reminded of their failures more than their successes. This creates an identity of failure.

The truth is very different. We are justified and declared innocent (Gal 2:16) and are entitled to a clean conscience (Heb 9:14). In fact the bible says that as far as the east is from the west, so far have our sins have been removed from us (Ps 103:12). What we have done in the past has no impact on who we are now and what we will do in the future. In fact we are also told that we are dead to sin but alive to God in Christ (Rom 6:11). Our identity has been changed from being a sinner to being righteous (2 Cor 5:21).

We are now called sons of God. We have been adopted into his family and sit at the right hand of God. Romans 8 describes the transformation we go through when we receive Jesus:

The Spirit you received does not make you slaves, so that you live in fear again; rather, the Spirit you received brought about your adoption to sonship. And by him we cry, "Abba, Father." The Spirit himself testifies with our spirit that we are God's children. Now if we are children, then we are heirs — heirs of God and co-heirs with Christ, if indeed we share in his sufferings in order that we may also share in his glory. (Rom 8:15-17)

Knowing that we are sons of God should give us a very different image of who we are. We are heirs to the throne who share in the glory of Christ! Too often we focus on our own personal failure or the generic failure of mankind and, in so doing, change our perception of who we are.

The mind-set of a son is very different from the mind-set of an orphan. Have a look at the table on the following page. In which areas are you a son and which areas do you have a tendency to think and act like an orphan?

You will notice that not all of the 'issues' this table looks at are only theological. Many of the issues, such as 'view of authority' apply to anyone in any context whether they know Jesus or not.

We need to be secure in our identity as sons and daughters. Once we become a son we are then qualified to father other sons back into a place of sonship, both in church and in the workplace. This isn't a one off event. There are always new levels of sonship that we can discover and move into. The revelation of our identity can always increase and we should always ask God to increase it.

The mind set of an Orphan	ISSUE	The mind set of Sons
God is a task master	**IMAGE OF GOD**	God is a loving Father and always good
Independent / Self-reliant	**DEPENDENCY**	Interdependent/Acknowledges need
Focus on the law	**THEOLOGY**	Focus on love
Strive for praise, approval and acceptance	**NEED FOR APPROVAL**	Totally accepted in God's love and justified by grace
A need for personal achievement as you seek to impress God and others, or no motivation to serve at all	**MOTIVE FOR SERVICE**	Service is motivated by a deep gratitude for being unconditionally loved and accepted by God
Duty or earning God's favour or no motivation at all	**MOTIVE BEHIND CHRISTIAN DISCIPLINES**	Pleasure and delight
Self-rejection from comparing yourself to others	**SELF-IMAGE**	Positive and affirmed because you know you have such value to God
Seek comfort in counterfeit affections: addictions, compulsions, escapism, busyness, hyper-religious activity	**SOURCE OF COMFORT**	Seek times of quietness and solitude to rest in the Father's presence and love
Competition, rivalry, and jealousy towards others' success and position	**PEER RELATIONSHIPS**	Humility and unity as you value others and are able to rejoice in their blessings and success
Accusation and exposure in order to make yourself look good by making others look bad	**HANDLING OTHERS' FAULTS**	Love covers as you seek to restore others in a spirit of love and gentleness
See authority as a source of pain: distrustful towards them and lack a heart attitude and submission	**VIEW OF AUTHORITY**	Respectful, honouring: see them as ministers of God for good in your life
Guarded and conditional: based upon others'performance as you seek to get your own needs met	**EXPRESSION OF LOVE**	Open, patient, and affectionate as you lay your life and agendas down in order to meet the needs of others
Conditional and distant	**SENSE OF GOD'S PRESENCE**	Close and intimate

adapted from Frost[3]

Who do we think we should be?

The culture in which we live is constantly trying to make us dissatisfied with our present circumstances; to want and expect more, in fact to believe that we deserve more. By doing a quick look back over the past few decades it is easy to see the change happening and the impact of it. Back in the sixties and seventies, if people couldn't afford something they saved up for it, now we buy it on credit and worry about paying it back later. We have all seen the impact this approach has had on society at large over the last six or seven years!

It can be hard to live in the now and find contentment with who we are and what we are doing now. However, living in the present and being present is so important. God didn't tell us to make disciples of all nations *when* we are ready, or *when* we have enough faith or *when* we are financially secure. The great commission is to do it now, to always do it. That isn't to say having vision, ambition and knowing that God is calling us into something else is bad, far from it. What isn't healthy though, is having such a focus on the future that we lose peace and contentment with who we are today and we put off doing what we should do today because we are waiting for tomorrow.

The more we allow this culture of dissatisfaction and entitlement to influence us, the greater the disconnect we create between who we are and who we think we should be.

We need to lead ourselves and others into a position of knowing our identity in Christ and the great things that come from sharing in his glory, whilst remaining content with who we are today and where we have been placed today.

The key to breakthrough is often acting in the opposite spirit to that which seems to control the culture. A controlling spirit in today's culture is an unhealthy focus on the future, dissatisfaction with the current state and entitlement. We need to redress this balance through humility and patience.

Humility

The world teaches us that we have rights. We have various rights that are protected by legislation, but more than that we have rights to the way we are treated and respected by others. We have rights to expect certain things in life and to expect a certain type of life. In other words we feel entitled to certain things and a certain way and level of life.

Philippians 2, as we have already seen, paints a very different story of our rights. Paul uses Jesus as an example of the only person who really did deserve to be treated differently and yet he chose to be a servant:

Who, being in very nature God, did not consider equality with God something to be used to his own advantage; rather, he made himself nothing by taking the very nature of a servant, being made in human likeness. And being found in appearance as a man, he humbled himself by becoming obedient to death – even death on a cross. (Phil 2: 6-8)

The result of Jesus making himself a servant is that *God exalted him to the highest place and gave him the name that is above every name, that at the name of Jesus every knee should bow, in heaven and on earth and under the earth* (Phil 2: 9-10).

The same happens to us when we become servants, we allow God to promote us and don't fall into the traps of vain conceit and self-ambition that we are warned about later on in Philippians 2. Falling into these traps is succumbing to the culture of today, of expecting more and living for our rights. Humility, as Jesus modelled, says I lay down the rights that the world says I should have. In fact accepting these earthly rights forfeits our heavenly rewards.

Patience

Patience is a very difficult quality to cultivate and is almost the exact opposite of the prevailing culture we live in. We expect to get things quickly and when we don't, we really struggle with it. However the bible tells us it is worth the wait:

Be patient, then, brothers and sisters, until the Lord's coming. See how the farmer waits for the land to yield its valuable crop, patiently waiting for the autumn and spring rains. ⁸ You too, be patient and stand firm, because the Lord's coming is near. ⁹Don't grumble against one another, brothers and sisters, or you will be judged. The Judge is standing at the door! (Jam 5: 7-9)

For the farmer to yield a good crop a combination of different qualities are needed: patience, hard work and an understanding of the seasons.

The farmer needs patience to wait for the rain, to plant at the right time and reap when the crops are ready. When it is time for action the farmer needs to work hard to seize the opportunity, but only when the time is right. I live in rural Norfolk and the farmers need to understand both their crop and the weather to know when to bring in the harvest. If they start bringing it in and the rains come their crop could be ruined. If they leave it too late and rains come, it could also be ruined. They need to read the seasons and know their crop.

I believe this is a prophetic picture for us and our leadership. We need to cultivate patience, we need to work hard and do our part but we also need to discern the heavenly perspective on situations so that we do the right thing at the right time. Patience prevents us from jumping the start with the 'good' rather than the 'best'.

What do others think about us?

The final part of Higgins' self-discrepancy theory is worrying about what others think of us. If we perceive a difference between who we think they think we are and who we think we are, then we can become negative towards ourselves. We need to worry less about other people and focus on what is right.

There are many verses in the bible that mention the fear of man and we won't study it in detail here other than to share Proverbs 29:25

Fear of man will prove to be a snare, but whoever trusts in the LORD is kept safe

Thinking about, worrying about and acting based on what

others think of us is not sustainable and will not lead us into the life God has for us. It will lead us into snares that stop us from walking in his promises and purpose.

We need to demonstrate, in our leadership, how to respect others, but not be driven by looking for their approval or respect. We need to be people of purpose who know what is right and stick to that course. That isn't to say we become dictators and don't take others' views into account. What I mean is we aren't swayed by what they think about us personally. It is far more important to know what God thinks about us!

Authority

Bandura's theory of self-efficacy[4] states that we limit ourselves by our own expectations. To put it simply; if we don't think we can achieve something then we are very unlikely to achieve it. I think it is perhaps easier to reflect on when the opposite is true, when we have a real deep down assurance we are going to succeed in something and that then comes to pass.

I particularly notice this phenomenon when playing golf, or rather trying badly to play golf. I stand at the ball with my club ready and I know before I swing the club whether it will be a good shot or whether I will fluff it. Why I know, I'm not sure. It could be because I am subconsciously working out whether I am standing correctly. It could be that actually the only thing that affects the shot is the thought in my head! If I think it will be a good shot, I relax and it generally is. If I think it will be a bad shot, I tense up and swing wrong. I don't know the reason, but I know it happens on multiple occasions when playing a round of golf. The more disconcerting thing is I still don't learn to stop the shot and start again when I do get these feelings!

A large amount of sports psychology is focused in this area; helping sports people believe that they have got what it takes to perform at the level required. In the work place the same phenomena is also very evident. People who 'make it' in work, whatever that means, are seldom those who don't know how they did and never thought they would. People who rise to the top in work, sports and other areas of life are usually those who have a deep self confidence in who they are and the ability that they have.

An interesting study has been done looking at young ice hockey players in Canada[5]. The study conclusively proved that children who had a birthday early in the school year are statistically far more likely to become a professional hockey player. The reason for this is as they are growing up they are the older kids in the year and therefore normally bigger than those whose birthday is later in the year. Size matters in hockey so in these early, formative years as a hockey player, they outperform those who are younger than them. Over time the physical difference disappears, but the self-confidence born from having out performed others remains. This results in a far higher proportion of those born early in the school year becoming professional in comparison to those born later in the school year.

Our expectations shouldn't be born from what we think we can achieve and who we think we are, but instead should be from who God says we are! Part of this comes from knowing our identity as we have looked at; the other side of the coin is understanding the authority that we have.

So what is our authority? As we've already seen in this chapter we are sons of God. That makes us royalty! When you are royal you have authority to make decisions that other, normal people, don't. This has to be our bedrock for looking at our authority; that we are heirs to the throne of heaven.

In Genesis 1, at the beginning of creation God gave dominion of the earth to humans forever.

Then God said, "Let us make mankind in our image, in our likeness, so that they may rule over the fish in the sea and the birds in the sky, over the livestock and all the wild animals, and over all the creatures that move along the ground."

So God created mankind in his own image, in the image of God he created them; male and female he created them. God blessed them and said to them, "Be fruitful and increase in number; fill the earth and subdue it. Rule over the fish in the sea and the birds in the sky and over every living creature that moves on the ground." (Gen1:26-28)

Dominion means that mankind was made the ruling authority over the earth. Adam had the right to use this authority in any way he chose. It was this authority that Satan wanted and that Adam passed over to Satan by falling for temptation. Interestingly the initial temptation by the Serpent in the Garden of Eden was actually based around identity because Satan knew that if he attacked our identity we would also forfeit our authority – what he is really after.

However, dominion of the earth and everything in it for mankind was always in God's plan. Psalm 115 says:

The highest heavens belong to the Lord, but the earth he has given to mankind. (Ps 115:16)

So Satan stole the governmental rule of the earth, but at the cross Jesus defeated Satan and bought back this authority. The only authority Satan now has is the authority that we give him by believing his lies and falling for his temptations. Satan has no right to this authority; Jesus won it back for us and triumphed over him.

And having disarmed the powers and authorities, he made a public spectacle of them, triumphing over them by the cross. (Col 2:15)

So we, mankind, now have this authority back because Jesus bought it back on the cross. We need to understand this truth and stand in it, as it is the truth that sets us free (Jn 8:32) and maintains our authority in the face of lies, accusations and temptations.

James says:

Submit yourselves, then, to God. Resist the devil, and he will flee from you. (Jam 4:7)

Knowing the truth that is in the Word of God is vital. If we know the truth, if we understand that the battle is won, that we are a new creation, that all authority has been delegated to us by Jesus and that our sins do not disqualify us because Jesus has already paid the price; then we can see the lies for what they are and reject and renounce them.

In fact our authority goes much further than just resisting and surviving. This is often the mind-set that Christians can adopt - survival until we get to heaven. Survival is not exercising our authority and dominion though and it certainly isn't living life in all of its fullness.

In the Gospel of Luke Jesus said:

I have given you authority to trample on snakes and scorpions and to overcome all the power of the enemy; nothing will harm you. (Lk 10:19)

Through Jesus we have authority over the spiritual realm as well as dominion over the earth. Christ, who now lives in us has won the war and will continue to win every battle that we face. This isn't just for the selected few 'special' believers. This is for all of us:

And these signs will accompany those who believe: In my name they will drive out demons; they will speak in new tongues; they will pick up snakes with their hands; and when they drink deadly poison, it will not hurt them at all; they will place their hands on sick people, and they will get well." (Mk16:17-18)

This passage depicts a very different Christian life to the experience I had growing up and I think the same is true for the majority of Christians. I've known that Jesus has the power to heal people, cast out demons and perform signs, wonders and miracles. I've also believed that I possibly might one day be part of Jesus performing such an act, but I certainly never believed or even understood that I had authority over the spiritual realms and should *expect* to do these things as I exercise my dominion over them. This was illustrated by the way I prayed. I prayed that Jesus would heal people rather than use my authority to command healing as Jesus taught the disciples.

It wasn't that I was actively taught that I didn't have this authority, but I think over time, the experience of the majority of Christians has led to a subtle watering down of our theology. At some point in time Christians weren't seeing signs, wonders and miracles follow them. This led to a shift in expectations and subtle changes in teaching. One of the most obvious ones can be seen in prayer ministry training in many churches. We are taught to pray that Jesus will heal people. In fact the bible tells _us_ to heal people (Mt 10:8). This progression can go further as you hear prayers that have somewhere in them 'if it's your will God then please heal this person'. This is theologically incorrect. God is good and is always good. He wants the kingdom of heaven to break out on earth with love and power. There is no sickness in heaven so he wants there to be none on earth. It is therefore always God's will to heal someone.

The authority to heal people, cast out demons and see the kingdom of heaven advance here on earth, has been given to all believers. We need to understand it, steward it and apply this, not just to our personal lives, but in all areas of life, so that through the authority given to us, we start to see heaven on earth as we were taught to pray in the Lord's Prayer. Living life in all its fullness can never just stop with us. It will always result in the transformation of others, of communities and of society at large.

The spiritual authority that we have will come under attack as it is this authority that Satan has been battling with mankind for since the beginning of time. The more we learn how to exercise the authority we have, the greater danger we become to the kingdom of darkness as we learn how to not just survive, but to take back what he has stolen and release others into a life of fullness. As I've heard said though; in the army Generals have a much greater level of protection than the foot soldiers!

This is especially true when we exercise our authority and take the kingdom of heaven into places that the church hasn't traditionally gone, notably the workplace. The divide between work and church has grown so wide that for many it seems like they have two lives. This is a lie from Satan. We are called to release the kingdom of heaven into the workplace and to set the captives free just as much as any other part of society. A lot of the consultancy work I am doing nowadays is releasing prophetic declarations and visions over organisations, just using friendly corporate language! The oppressions and problems in many of our large corporations are demonic in nature and understanding the spiritual realm and exercising authority in this sphere is the only way to solve the problems of the organisation and to set the captive workers free to fulfil the potential they have and to live life to the full.

I have come across many people who consciously don't engage in the spiritual realm of our faith because of a fear that they will come under greater attack if they do. This position of fear then stops them walking in the fullness that comes from understanding the authority we have been given, let alone the righteousness, peace and joy that are characteristics of life with the Holy Spirit. This fear is founded on the lies of the enemy and as a result, causes poor thinking and decision making. Timothy was warned against this in Paul's letter to him. I like the Amplified translation as it really describes what the fear is like:

For God did not give us a spirit of timidity (of cowardice, of craven and cringing and fawning fear), but [He has given us a spirit] of power and of love and of calm and well-balanced mind and discipline and self-control. (2 Tim1:7)

The fear stops the sound mind and also stops us acting in power. Believing the lies that lead to fear is actually even more serious in the context of our pursuit of a full life. Verse six of this passage says: *...I remind you to fan into flame the gift of God that is in you...for God did not give us a spirit of timidity...* So if we succumb to fear it stops the gift of God in us being fanned into flame. Using the gifts God has given us is part of walking in the calling we have and living a full life. Fear actively stops us from living a revived and full life as Jesus intended.

We know that fear comes from a lie as the bible is very clear about it. Firstly, the passage in Timothy says it doesn't come from God and if it isn't from God and is trying to steal our giftings and destiny away from us, then there is only one other place it can have come from. We have full authority over Satan and as such he has no legal right to torment us in this way.

He who is in us is greater than he who is in the world (1 Jn4:4)

The reason the Son of God appeared was to destroy the devil's work (1 Jn3:8)

Jesus destroyed the works of the devil and now lives in us as the greatest authority. Tormenting us, lying to us and putting fear in us are exactly the works of the devil that Jesus came to destroy. Through the delegated authority we have of Christ in us, we are able to take authority over them and rebuke them for what they are.

The characteristics of the Holy Spirit are righteousness, peace and joy (Rom14:17), so when the Holy Spirit is in us and we are working in the power of the spirit, these characteristics will also be seen in us. Peace is a characteristic that goes hand in hand with walking and operating in our authority. One of Bill Johnson's famous quotes is that *'you only have authority over the storm you can sleep in'.* He is referring to Jesus sleeping in the storm whilst his disciples are panicking (Mt 8:23-27). The disciples wake him up; he then calms the storms before having some pretty harsh words for the disciples' lack of faith.

When we are sure and confident of our authority we have peace about situations that seemingly have no peace attached to them. When we feel that peace it reminds us of our authority to calm the storm.

My firm has been involved in a large and strategically significant (for us anyway) EU contract. The contract is research and development to identify and explore the barriers that stop women progressing into senior management positions. It is being run across the UK and France with my company as the lead partner and a French company as a junior partner to the project.

I haven't been involved in the day to day running of the project, but have ultimate accountability for it. There had been some teething problems with the partnership and particularly with the payment terms from the EU who are used to paying large institutions not small companies who care about their cash flow! On a Thursday, I was about to go into a meeting with another client before heading over to a weekend long intervention with 35 English and French participants. Just as I was going into the meeting, an email came through from the French partner raising concerns about the programme that I knew nothing about. They finished off the email by threatening to pull out of the programme which would have had major ramifications.

This could have been very significant, not just for the success of the project, but also for the company as a whole as it could have raised the prospect of the EU clawing back all payments as a result of not finishing the project. I should have felt stressed and nervous, but for some reason I had complete peace about the situation and complete assurance that God was going to move in sovereign power.

I arranged to meet with the CEO of the French partner the following day to talk through the issues, knowing that, not only would the situation be resolved, but that peace and joy would extend through me and be released across the partnership and particularly that weekend's events.

That is exactly what happened. My meeting with the French partner lasted only 10 minutes. It was a fantastic meeting. I was able to honour her, act in humility and reassure her that things would work well from this point on. She accepted this far quicker than her track record suggested she would and joy and peace were passed on to her. This quickly spread across the whole group and by the end of the weekend, everyone there was commenting on the strength of the relationships formed, the joy they had experienced and the peace they felt about the rest of the work.

They don't all know the reason for this. But that's the point. God loves all of us whether we know him yet or not and he loves for his kingdom to impact on everyone. As a son of his I was able to extend the grace he showed me to other people and to change the spiritual atmosphere to victory from a situation that originally had defeat written all over it.

Our spiritual authority is completely based upon our union with Jesus. Ephesians 1 demonstrates how God gave full authority to Jesus and through our relationship with him, we also have this authority.

I keep asking that the God of our Lord Jesus Christ, the glorious Father, may give you the Spirit of wisdom and revelation, so that you may know him better. I pray that the eyes of your heart may be enlightened in order that you may know the hope to which he has called you, the riches of his glorious inheritance in his holy people, and his incomparably great power for us who believe. That power is the same as the mighty strength ʰᵉ exerted when he raised Christ from the dead and seated him at his right hand in the heavenly realms, far above all rule and authority, power and dominion, and every name that is invoked, not only in the present age but also in the one to come. And God placed all things under his feet and appointed him to be head over everything for the church, which is his body, the fullness of him who fills everything in every way. (Eph1:17-23)

As a body of believers we have the fullness of the sovereign authority that God gave to Jesus – wow. We need to learn what this authority really means and how to steward it.

Faith

Faith plays a big part in authority, or at least exercising our authority. In Matthew 10 the disciples are sent out to heal the sick, cast out demons, cleanse lepers and raise the dead and they did this. Then in Matthew 17 we hear about a father who comes to Jesus because the disciples failed to cast a demon out of his child. Jesus casts out the demons and frees the little boy. The disciples ask him why they didn't manage to do the same. Jesus replied to them: *"Because you have so little faith. Truly I tell you if you have faith as small as a mustard seed you can say to this mountain move from here to there and it will move. Nothing will be impossible for you"* (Mt17:20-21).

So the reason the disciples weren't able to cast out the demon was because they lacked faith. They had had it, they had understood their authority and walked in it, but for some reason, in that particular circumstance, they lacked faith and the result of that was the little girl wasn't healed.

The same happens to us and we must contend for more faith. It is a gift from God and we must continually ask for more and position ourselves to increase our faith by reminding ourselves of previous victories as the Israelites did in the Old Testament.

Why the disciples lacked faith at that particular point, I don't know for sure, but I wonder if it is linked to some of what we read in the previous chapter. In chapter 16 Jesus warns them against the yeast of the Pharisees and the Sadducees. The yeast of the Pharisees is the religious spirit and by calling it yeast Jesus is saying that if a small amount is let in, it can grow and multiply and affect everything.

The religious spirit is looking for rules, for formulas, for control and for hierarchy. This can easily creep into our thinking in very subtle ways; "the way we pray for people round here is like this...". Jesus didn't heal anyone the same way twice. Control is at the heart of the religious spirit. This is the opposite of the Holy Spirit who is freedom. If we allow control to creep in it can quench the spirit and stop the power being released into a situation.

Stewardship

We need to learn how to steward our authority so that it grows and increases. This is a biblical principle of the kingdom. We are told that the kingdom of heaven is like a mustard seed that grows into a large tree (Lk 13:19). The parable of the talents (Mt 25:14-30) also tells us that Jesus wants us to invest what we have and see increase.

However the normal approach is often the opposite. We exercise authority once, get used to that and at some point in the future do the same thing again. We must increase our level of authority by stewarding it and growing the authority that we are walking in. Alan Scott, leader of Causeway Coast Vineyard, puts is as follows: "we're not after moments, we are after momentum".

I was at a small funfair with my children recently and I got a picture of what it means to steward not just our authority, but the kingdom of heaven that lives inside of us. The first ride in the park was the snails. This was a two person ride where you sat on a snail that went round a race track. My eldest daughter, who was nine at the time, had an enormous grin on her face and she loved the ride. After the snails we went further into the park and found increasingly bigger and better rides that made my kid's adrenaline flow in increasingly greater measures. We came towards the end of the pre-paid tokens we had bought and there was only enough for one more ride each. The girls decided they would go on the snails again because they had enjoyed them so much at the beginning of the day. They went on them and my eldest daughter was incredibly disappointed. They weren't as good as she remembered and she felt like she had wasted her last ride.

The reason they weren't as good was because she had experienced better and going back to the snails just didn't give her the same buzz. I think we often have a ride on the snails, go out of the park, come back in a few weeks later and then go on the snails again. We don't push in further; we don't steward these moments and turn them into momentum as we grow in the authority we are walking in. We have to become dissatisfied with the snails and push on for more. The snails become our floor not our ceiling. We steward the authority we have and look for a higher ceiling.

So what – what to do with it?

So we have authority. What can we do with our authority to release life into our churches and businesses?

1. Teach on authority and model it – in churches it is vital to teach all believers about the authority they have and why they have it. In business, upfront teaching on this may not be possible but you can model the characteristics that come from authority; namely righteousness, peace and joy in the Holy Spirit. As people see these characteristics as part of you, despite circumstances, you will start to release the same characteristics to others.

2. Pursue friendship with Jesus – Peter had the keys of the kingdom (authority) passed on to him through his friendship with Jesus and the same is true for us (see chapter 12)

3. Spend time asking Jesus to reveal the secrets of heaven and the spiritual dynamics at play in churches and workplaces so that you know what to take authority over; what to bind and loose in heaven and earth (Mt 16:19)

4. Build your faith in the authority that you carry by contending for it and asking Jesus to increase the measure of faith that you have

5. Steward the authority you carry. When you have a 'moment' of authority actively look for increase from there and take risks to get increase. By doing this we get the return on investment that Jesus is looking for from the investment he has made in us.

Balancing Expectations

In the work I have done in large organisations there seems to be a tipping point for leading other people's expectations. If we expect too much of them we overwhelm them and decrease their engagement. However, often we hold people back; we don't allow them to flourish or use their strengths and giftings and as a result, their self-expectations are greater than their ability to use their strengths and giftings. This also decreases engagement.

As leaders we have to find the tipping point. We need to push people who need pushing beyond their expectations, whilst supporting them. We also need to help develop character in others whilst empowering them towards their expectations.

References

1. Higgins, E. T. (1987). Self-discrepancy: A theory relating self and affect. Psychological Review, 94, 319- 340.

2. Bickle, M. (2011) After God's Own Heart: The Key to Knowing and Living God's Passionate Love for You. Charisma House

3. Adapted from Frost, Jack (2007) Spiritual Slavery to Spiritual Sonship, Destiny Image

4 Bandura, A. (1977). Self-efficacy: Toward a unifying theory of behavioural change. Psychological Review, 84(2), 191-215.

5.http://www.plosone.org/article/info%3Adoi%2F10.1371%2Fjournal.pone.0 057753.

8

Overcoming Loss and Fear

I've worked on, and been involved in, many change projects both in the workplace and in churches. They rarely seem to go smoothly as they are times of such heightened emotions. There was a particular project I was working on in which I came across a lady called Jeanette. She worked for an NHS Trust that was going through a fairly major change and reorganisation programme. She was a junior manager and had understood the need for the change and the logic and rationale behind the way it was being done. However she couldn't get her heart around it even though she understood it in her head.

After spending some time with her it emerged there were two main issues: the fact that what she was losing in the process, or that she perceived she was losing, was more important to her than the benefits of the programme at that particular point in time. Secondly, the uncertainty that the change created was very unsettling for her. She was losing a support network of people she had grown to know and trust. As part of the change she was moving to a different part of the building to work with people she didn't know too well. It was probably a good opportunity for her, with greater career prospects, and she knew that. However, it seemed the logical, rational benefits were outweighed by the sense of loss she was also experiencing.

To lead others into fullness of life we need to understand how and why people respond to change in the way they do and in fact we need to understand why we respond in the way that we do!

I've called this chapter loss and fear because I believe they are actually dealing with the same issue. When working with secular organisations I use the term loss, but the reason loss is a big issue for people is usually because of fear. Our fear is often based on our assessment of the risks involved and what we stand to gain and loose. Jeanette was affected by the loss of the team she was working with because she feared she wouldn't create the same level of trusting relationship with the new team she would be part of.

Kahneman and Tversky[1] pioneered a particularly psychological theory called Prospect Theory that has since been the subject of many rigorous studies. Their findings have withstood the test of these studies and give us some interesting insights into the way humans work. The main principles behind prospect theory are:

Certainty: People have a strong preference for certainty and are willing to sacrifice potential gain to achieve more certainty. For example, if option A is a guaranteed win of £1,000, and option B is an 80 percent chance of winning £1,400 but a 20 percent chance of winning nothing, people tend to prefer option A.

Loss aversion: People tend to give losses more weight than gains — they're loss averse. So, if you gain £100 and lose £80, it may be considered a net *loss* in terms of satisfaction, even though you came out £20 ahead, because you'll tend to focus on how much you lost, not on how much you gained.

Understanding our desire for certainty, the fact we are loss averse and the impact fear has on us, gives us further clues about living life to the full and leading others into fullness.

Certainty

Consistency and certainty are strong driving forces in us humans. We want to know where we stand financially, in our relationships and in our work. Society is structured around having this kind of consistency and certainty. Most of us have a regular monthly salary that is needed to pay the regular monthly mortgage and other regular monthly bills. We budget based on our regular monthly income and outgoings. We hope for security in our jobs so that we can commit to these regular monthly commitments. We look to give certainty and consistency for our children by not moving around too much so they can stay in the same school etc.

None of this is wrong and in fact, more often than not, is based on good wisdom and is an example of good stewardship of the things we have been given; money, resources and a family. However, it is also important to see it for what it is; a strong psychological desire to base our decision making on certainty rather than risk.

Making conservative decisions because of the need for certainty is hard wired into our thinking. I am obviously generalising here and there are many people who buck this trend, however, for the majority of the population, this is how we think.

Whilst there is much wisdom and good stewardship that comes from this way of thinking, it also creates major problems when trying to change; individually and in workplaces and churches. The reason it creates these problems is because our certainty is based largely on our experiences and therefore doesn't allow for there to be a greater reality than our own experiences.

In organisations, both churches and workplaces, one of the largest factors that we come up against when trying to help implement a programme of change, is that people have already made up their mind about whether a programme will work or not. This position is largely created from their experiences of previous change programmes, either in their current organisation or in past ones. These experiences create expectations, both for the programme overall, and for the individual's own reaction to the change programme. As we have seen in the chapter on self-expectations, this sets the limit to their expected experience of the current change programme. Put simply, if someone thinks the change is rubbish, will be done badly and affect them emotionally, that is probably the way they will relate to the change programme because that is their expectation of it from the beginning.

I've seen this happen in many workplaces and in some churches. Our current church has been revitalised over the last couple of years through a partnership with Holy Trinity Brompton (HTB) in London. We started going a couple of months before Ian and Jo Dyble came from HTB and, in doing so, got to know some of the original congregation. They had had four church leaders in the last 10 years which led a number of them to the following attitude to Ian and Jo coming: "we were here before the last four Vicars, we will be here after this Vicar leaves and therefore we will weather the storm of change that the new Vicar will bring in (because all the others tried to change things so I'm sure this one will as well) and it will eventually go away"!

In many workplaces people have been so hurt by their previous experiences of change that the mere thought of it conjures up powerful emotions that are far stronger than rational thought and logic.

One of the most interesting parts of the example of certainty given at the beginning of this chapter is the perceived chance of winning nothing. In the example there was the chance of turning £1,000 into £1,400 but there was also a 20% chance of winning nothing. The percentage chance of winning nothing or losing is a judgement call we make and is coloured by our experiences. For example someone could think "my experience of the last change I went through was that it was done badly so I think the chance of winning nothing is 50% not 20%". Our perception of winning nothing, of being affected badly, is based on a judgement call that comes from our experiences.

The same is true when thinking about taking risks to do with our faith. The percentage chance of 'winning nothing' is largely based on our previous experiences and our theology. For example I could think; "I won't pray for that person on crutches in the street because my experience tells me that my chance of 'not winning' and them not being healed is pretty high, so despite the fact it would be amazing if it did happen, I'm not going to do it. What's more I could look like a fool, what would people think of me?"

Does this pattern of thinking sound familiar? We perceive two areas of loss in this equation: firstly that the healing won't happen and secondly that others will think you are an idiot. This perception of loss reduces our perceived chance of winning and increases the attractiveness of maintaining the status quo and not stepping out and taking a risk.

The same goes for our attitude towards evangelism, giving, making life changing decisions to follow God down a particular path or calling and taking steps to see the Kingdom extend into our workplaces and communities.

The subconscious decision making process we go through tells us that the certainty we have in doing things the way we have always done them, is stronger than the potential increase we will get by taking a risk.

Other research undertaken suggests that the potential gain has to be twice that of the potential loss for people to consider the risk worth taking. In the experiment people were given a 50/50 chance of either winning or losing money. People would only take that chance if the amount they might win was worth twice the value of what they might lose.

Two ways of looking at this

There are two ways of looking at this equation to redress it so we see it from a heavenly perspective rather than through our lens of looking for certainty.

The first is to address our theology so we get a better understanding of what the potential rewards are and the faithfulness of God. This reduces the risk as we quickly see the chance of losing is greatly diminished! By looking at things this way the equation changes which in turn changes the decisions we make.

There are three parts to the equation:

- The value we place on what we already have (let's call that V)
- The perceived value of what we might get (let's call that P)
- The percentage chance of losing (let's call that L)

Therefore there are three ways of changing this equation; decreasing the value we place on the current situation (V), increasing the value we place on what we might get (P) and decreasing the percentage chance of losing (L).

All three of these happen when understanding how good God is and how he wants the Kingdom extended far more than we do!

V decreases when we get a better understanding of God's plans for us to prosper personally and for his plans, purposes and promises for the future; this also makes P increase. L decreases when we increase our faith, understand the authority that we have and understand more about the faithfulness of God.

Obviously if this change in theology, or at the least the application of theology to our thought patterns, is matched with increasing experiences of the results of taking risks of faith then it is a very strong combination!

When you do get results by stepping out in faith, write them down and remember them. Use them as ways to remember the victories you have had when co-labouring with God. It will increase your faith and change the equation further.

The other way of looking at this is completely different. It says that this equation put forward by Kahneman and Tversky doesn't follow the same rules as the kingdom of God. In the kingdom of God, as risk goes up so does the chance of winning! This doesn't fit our thought patterns because this shouldn't happen! In our world, as risk increases the chances of winning decrease, but not in the kingdom!

The more we take risks and step out in faith, the more we are giving God the opportunity to show his love and his power and do you know what – he loves to do that. By actually stepping out in faith and taking risk we increase the chance of winning!

We need to constantly remind ourselves of this because it is counter intuitive. Our experience, society and the hard wiring of our brains tells us the opposite. The truth is though, in the kingdom, as you take the risk you are also increasing your chance of a massive pay out!

Exodus 16 gives us a wonderful picture of how the Israelites natural need for certainty is at complete contrasts with God's plans. God provides manna and quails for the Israelites for them to eat during their time in the desert, but he did this with specific instructions:

Then the Lord said to Moses, "I will rain down bread from heaven for you. The people are to go out each day and gather enough for that day. In this way I will test them and see whether they will follow my instructions. On the sixth day they are to prepare what they bring in, and that is to be twice as much as they gather on the other days (Ex16: 4-5).

God provided them enough for each day, but as a test of faith and obedience, he didn't allow them to gather in more than they needed for that one day. Some of the Israelites then proved just how strong their hard wired need for certainty was. They gathered more than they needed for one day to store for future use:

Then Moses said to them, "No one is to keep any of it until morning."

However, some of them paid no attention to Moses; they kept part of it until morning, but it was full of maggots and began to smell. So Moses was angry with them (Ex16: 19-20).

I think it is easy to read this passage and think, stupid people; didn't they listen to the instructions? Why didn't they just do what God and Moses told them to do? Whilst that is true, I think it is also easy to see why they didn't. Collecting more than we need for today to save it for hard times is sensible. There seems to be wisdom in it and it is good stewardship. In fact there are stories in the bible that prove this; Joseph interpreted a dream telling the Pharaoh to store up food for seven years ready for a famine. However this isn't real wisdom, it is fear and the need for certainty masquerading as wisdom. Wisdom is following God's instruction in every situation. Joseph did this, but it was a different instruction for the Israelites in the desert. The power of the Israelite's hard wired thought processes; to look for certainty and their fear of uncertainty, overpowered them, reduced their faith and led to disobedience.

Exactly the same is true for us. True wisdom is seeing things from God's perspective. Paul, in his letter to the Ephesians asks that God will give them the spirit of wisdom and revelation (Eph 1:17). This shows us that real wisdom comes from God and is linked to revelation about God's plans and purposes. All too often we don't take the opportunities to practice our faith in him under the guise of wisdom. It isn't wisdom at all, it is allowing our need for certainty to create fear for the uncertain which stops us seeing the potential return that God has for us.

Loss Aversion

The other part of Prospect Theory, loss aversion, is interesting as it provides another insight into human nature. An interesting experiment was done in London's Spitalfields Market by the BBC programme Horizon. Strangers were approached and given £20 and offered the chance to increase that to £50 by betting it against a roulette wheel.

This was the basic scenario, but it was put to people in two different ways. In the first scenario people were given £20 and told they could stick with the £20 or they could use it to bet and possibly turn it into £50. The vast majority of people approached using this method, stuck with the £20.

The second way people were approached was slightly different. They were given £50 and immediately had £30 taken away. They were told they could win it back by betting the £20 they still had. Looking at this rationally it is the same scenario. People ended up with £20 they didn't have before and were told they could either keep it or use it to gamble with to possibly gain another £30.

However, because of the different way the scenario was put to the people, the results were totally different. One group had the full £50 in their hands to begin with, so when £30 was taken away from them they felt they had lost something. The majority of people approached using this scenario decided to gamble the money compared to a very small percentage of people approached using the other scenario.

Most people are more concerned about keeping what they've got than gaining something they have never had. We worry more about loss than gain. As leaders we must be aware of this in ourselves so we don't pass God given opportunities for promotion over. We also must be aware of this in the way we lead our people.

We need a kingdom mindset with minds renewed and

transformed to see opportunities from God's eyes not from human nature. We also need to understand the way our congregations and workforces think. It doesn't work just talking about the potential gain; we also have to increase dissatisfaction with the current position.

Fear

It is often because of the seed of fear that we allow wisdom based on human nature to gain precedence over God given wisdom and revelation.

Fear is the enemy of you living a life of fullness and of leading others into that same life. As we have already seen, Paul specifically warns Timothy about the affect fear can have:

For this reason I remind you to fan into flame the gift of God, which is in you through the laying on of my hands. For the Spirit God gave us does not make us timid, but gives us power, love and self-discipline　　　　　　　　　　　　　　　　　(2Tim1:6-7).

There are many potential sources of fear for a leader: a lack of self-confidence, imposter syndrome (feeling that you are a fake and blagging it), a culture in your work environment of coming down hard on failure, tough market conditions that make every decision vital, a worry for the future or worry of what others will think of you.

We need to be able to overcome this fear as fear is not of God and, as the passage in 2 Timothy shows us; it reduces power, love, self-control and stops the gift of God that is in us from being fanned into flames. Sometimes removing fear can be a process that we work through rather than it being an instantaneous event (although it certainly can be that). In fact it seems that this was the case for Timothy or else Paul wouldn't have had to write to him to remind him about it. A good staging post for dealing with fear is to focus on stopping the symptoms of fear affecting our leadership.

By focusing on stopping the symptoms of fear we will, over time, change our habitual way of thinking and reduce the impact of fear on our leadership.

The symptoms of fearful leadership

We disempower others as our power decreases - the leader takes more and more upon their own shoulders as they don't trust others to achieve the same results they could or because they feel threatened by gifted people in their congregation or workplaces. This decreases engagement by reducing involvement and autonomy. Empowering others to use and develop their gifts and strengths and involving others in key decisions are all motivating factors that increase engagement in workforces and, in so doing, move people towards living a full life. Giving others autonomy is also proven to be a highly motivating factor, whilst disempowering staff reduces their involvement and autonomy. One of the personal characteristics of engaging leaders is that they are trustworthy and they trust others. The likelihood is that trust is also undermined by disempowering others.

The strength of relationships decrease as our love decreases – when the leader draws everything closer to themselves and are less trusting and authentic in their relationships, it decreases engagement by reducing trust in the relationship and changing the values of the relationship. Trust is again the main characteristic that will be eroded by succumbing to fear in leadership. Followers will feel they aren't trusted and in turn the trust they have in their leader will decrease. A change in the strength of relationship says quite a bit about the values, particularly the informal values that are evident in the workplace or congregation. When we see alignment between our personal values and the formal and informal values of the workplace or congregation we are more engaged and more a part of it. The converse is also true!

The quality of decisions decreases as our self-control decreases - the leader's emotional intelligence is reduced and they have less awareness of the impact they have on others, less empathy with others and less self-control. This decreases engagement by reducing trust and hope. We also become less stable in the way we respond to people as our self-control is reduced, which again decreases their engagement and connection. When emotional intelligence is reduced, our ability to control ourself is also reduced, leading to instability. Hope and compassion; two other important characteristics of engaging leaders also decrease as fear affects decision making.

The impact of fearful leadership

An obvious impact on people when fear becomes a part of our decision making is a reduction in engagement and connection. This becomes a vicious cycle; as fear increases, connection drops further which reinforces this unhealthy loop. The less obvious impact is that we never become the leader we could be. We don't reach our potential and have the impact we could have because we are hamstrung by letting fear affect our thinking.

The passage in Timothy is so important in understanding many of the problems that exist in the workplace and in some of our congregations. These verses tell us that fear is the opposite of power, love and self-control. This means that fear is also the opposite of the behaviours of; empowering others, building strong and good relationships and of good emotional intelligence. To have power and be powerful is to give it away and empower others. To demonstrate love in the workplace is to build good relationships. Self-control or high levels of emotional intelligence have been shown by Daniel Goleman to be the main distinguishing factor that separates great leaders with average leaders.[2] Staff not being empowered by defensive leaders, relationships breaking down and leaders who lack self-control and awareness of the impact they have on others, are three of the most common problems I see across businesses of all types and are some of the main reasons there are unfulfilled captives in our workforces. The root of this is fear, which isn't from God. We need to take authority over fear in our workplaces and release power, love and self-control as the normal ways of operating.

To live in the fullness of life and to lead others into it, we must recognise that there are some patterns of thought that are natural to us, which are actually counter-productive to living a full life in the kingdom. The effect of fear impacting on our thinking and decision making is made clear in the letter to Timothy. If we let fear creep in then the gift of God that is in us won't be fanned into flame. The result of this gift is life in all its fullness! Therefore fear is the great enemy of a full life.

The following two check lists are to help you reflect on how loss aversion, the need for certainty and fear affect your thinking and decision making.

As you read through them ask the Holy Spirit to highlight any deep or hidden areas of fear that affect you and your leadership. If you find any, renounce them in the name of Jesus and invite the Holy Spirit to deepen your faith in God to replace the fear.

Personal check list

		Yes	No
1	Do you perceive the future based on your past experiences?		
2	Do your experiences align to the goodness, power and love of God?		
3	Is the value you are placing on the status quo right and healthy?		
4	Do you see the possibilities through Gods eyes?		
5	How powerful is the fear of losing and how likely do you think loss is?		
6	Do you focus more on loss or gain?		
7	Is fear masquerading as wisdom?		

Leading others check list

1	How are past experiences affecting expectations of the future?	
2	How can you increase dissatisfaction with the status quo?	
3	How can you create an empowering culture?	
4	How can you strengthen relationships thorough a culture of love?	
5	How can you make better decisions through good self-control and increase emotional intelligence across the organisation	
6	How can you create a prophetic culture so the wisdom you have is from God and drawn from revelation?	

References

1. Kahneman, Daniel, and <u>Amos Tversky</u>. "Prospect Theory: An Analysis of Decision Under Risk". *Econometrica*. XLVII (1979): 263–291.
2. Daniel Goleman (1995) Emotional Intelligence, why it matters more than IQ.

9

Personal Characteristics of Leaders / Fathering

It is easy to see how our personal characteristics impact on how others are released into fullness of life, of reaching their potential and being engaged or revived. In the workplace, the culture we create through our example and the decisions we make have direct consequences in others' lives and therefore impact on the way they are able to live in fullness.

The research our firm has done has found the leadership culture that exists in organisations to be the single biggest factor that impacts on engagement. This means it is also the biggest factor influencing the productivity of the organisation and the quality of life of the employees / members. This culture is set by us, the leaders.

In the church it is also easy to see the impact leaders have on others' destiny. Do leaders help people to find their calling and empower and equip them into it, or do we create conditions for them to serve our calling, ministry and vision?

As leaders, we are fathers and mothers to others. Fathers and mothers create the culture of their families and create the conditions for their children to grow. Good fathers and mothers release their children to grow and flourish by providing a loving and stable base and supporting their children to be all that they can be. When we lead as fathers rather than leaders, we create the conditions for those who follow us to grow and flourish. A father does whatever they can to see their children surpass them.

Our personal characteristics are important, not just to release others into fullness of life, but so we can have life in all its fullness as well. We have been made in the image of God, who is our Father, so for us to be living in all he has for us, we need to understand some of the characteristics of our Father God and see them in our lives.

Ensuring our dominant characteristics are close to those of our Father; who is the best at releasing us into our destiny and who sent his Son so that we could have life in all of its fullness, is vital. So what are those characteristics?

Some really interesting research has been undertaken by Gallup looking at the personal characteristics of leaders that have the most engaged followers. Their premise is that to find out what leadership characteristics engage people, the ones to ask are not the leaders, but the followers of leaders. What is it about their leaders that engages or disengages them?

They conducted this research globally between 2005 and 2008, initially with around 10,000 people, creating a strong and robust research base to draw conclusions from. They asked people to think of a leader that has the most positive effect on their daily life and then to think of what this person contributes to their life.[1] They concluded there are four characteristics that are more important than any others in engaging followers. Engaged followers means two things, firstly that they are enjoying their work; that they are closer to living in the fullness. Secondly, that they are more productive so the organisation, of whatever type, achieves more.

The four characteristics they found to be so important are; *trust*, *hope*, *compassion* and *stability*. We will break them down and look at each one shortly to see what they mean, what the research said, what the bible says about them and then what we can do to demonstrate these characteristics in our lives. However, before doing that let's have a look at these characteristics in the context of one of the most famous parables of the bible, a parable all about the characteristics of a good father.

The parable of the Prodigal Son

This parable has been given the title of the parable of the prodigal son, but it is far more about the father than it is the son. The parable starts off with the son demanding what he should really only receive once his father was dead. *'Father, give me my share of the estate'.* (Lk15:12) This would be similar to him saying; "Dad, you'd be far more use to me if you were dead as what I want from you I will only receive when you are dead". Not a particularly nice thing for a son to say to his father. However, despite this, the father did as he was asked, he divided his property between his two sons and, by doing so, he released his son, giving him the freedom to find his own way.

Shortly after this the son leaves and squanders all of his inheritance in distant lands. It is quite likely that the father heard nothing from him and didn't know what was happening to him.

When his son came back, the father is still extravagant in his love. He sees him while he is still a long way off and is filled with compassion for him (Lk15:20). He runs to meet him, throws his arms around him and kisses him. He restores him to his place as son and heir in the eyes of others, in the eyes of the family and in the eyes of the son himself. The whole story is about love and full restoration, not just restoration from a bad place to an average place. Sometimes we might think; "I've been bad perhaps God will forgive my sins enough that I can get into heaven and church"! No, this story is about the full restoration of the son's birth rights as heir to his father.

The father asks the servant to:

Quick! Bring the best robe and put it on him. Put a ring on his finger and sandals on his feet. Bring a fattened calf and kill it. Let's have a feast and celebrate. For this son of mine was dead and is alive again; he was lost and is found.' (Lk15:22-24)

Culturally it was very important for the father to publicly restore the son. In the passage above we see that; by giving the son the best robe he restored his position, by giving him a ring he restored his authority and by giving him sandals he restored him as a son. He then continued to be extravagant and had a feast to celebrate. The father didn't hold back. He didn't hold anything against his son and he didn't let hurt or offence impact on the way he responded to his son. He extravagantly loved him throughout the whole story.

So do the characteristics, identified by Gallup, play out in the parable? I think they really do.

Trust – The father shows that he is not only trustworthy, he is also trusting. He trusts his son and gives him his inheritance when the son asks for it. By trusting his son he empowers and releases him, setting the foundation that makes it possible for the son to return later on. It is the father's trustworthiness that becomes the trigger for the son to come back. He thinks; *'how many of my fathers hired men have food to spare, and here I am starving to death! I will set out and go back to my father and say to him: Father I have sinned against heaven and against you. I am no longer worthy to be called your son; make me like one of your hired men.'* (Lk15:17-19)

The son sees that the father can be trusted because of the way he provides for his staff. The son must have observed this for many years whilst growing up in the family household. The track record of being trustworthy created the conditions for the son to come back. Once the son does return he quickly finds out that his father could be trusted way beyond his expectations!

Hope – throughout the story the father gives hope to the son. He gives hope at the beginning of the story by giving the son his inheritance so the son could live the life that he hoped for.

While the son was starving and feeding pigs, the father was his source of hope and when he returned, the father restored the son's hope fully by reinstating him in the family.

Compassion – the father demonstrates deep compassion for the son. The fact he saw his son, whilst he was still a long way off, suggests he might have been looking for him, probably driven by worry and compassion. Verse 20 tells us the father was filled with compassion when he saw his son and ran to him, breaking many cultural barriers in doing so. One of the characteristics of this compassion is it is focused far more on the son's need than the fathers feelings. The father's emotions and feelings of hurt, anger and rejection aren't even mentioned and compassion for the well-being of the son is absolutely paramount. The father didn't hold anything against the son, there was no trial period or probation. The compassion of the father restored this son immediately.

Stability – the father was the same at the beginning of this story as he was at the end. At the beginning he was extravagant in his love and empowering in his nature and he was exactly the same at the end of the story when the son returned.

So a good father is trusting and trustworthy. Good fathers give hope through the way they empower and the decisions they make. A good father is compassionate and puts the needs of others above their own insecurities. A good father is stable and constant and gives stability to others through this.

This parable is about restoring someone to live the life they were always meant to live. Surely this is one of the key tasks for us as leaders of businesses, churches and families. If we restore others to the life they were always meant to live, then we are also living the life we are meant to live, we are revived and living in the fullness.

These four characteristics have been shown by research from Gallup and in the parable of the Prodigal Son to be very important in empowering others to live life in all its fullness and in living that type of life ourselves. But what does that mean in reality? What does it look like to have these characteristics prominent in our lives, work and ministry? How can we improve in these areas and what are some of the barriers that we might come up against? The rest of this chapter will look at these characteristics in more depth to explore what we can all do to develop these characteristics and the results this will have.

Trust

Gallup found the chances of an employee being engaged at work if they don't trust the company's leaders is 1 in 12. However the chances of an employee being engaged if they do trust the company's leaders are better than 1 in 2. This is more than a six fold increase and will have a corresponding impact on productivity, performance and the life that the employee is living.

So what is it that leads to trust or in fact distrust. At a very obvious level if the leader is a liar or found to be unethical in the decisions they make, then trust is eroded. However the picture is actually far more complex than that. I'm sure many of you have worked with leaders who have the best intentions and want to give the best results for their staff. The result of this is they can often over promise. They say they will do things and have the best intentions to do them, but never quite deliver against what they say they will do. This might come from a good place, but actually the effect is the same; trust is eroded. The call to leaders towards integrity and trust is a prophetic one at this time.

Stephen M.R. Covey, in his book; The Speed of Trust identifies four key components of trust: integrity, intent, capability and results. The first two are internal factors that others judge us by whilst the second two relate to our performance and whether others will trust us to do a certain task based on their perception of our ability and track record.

Every year Edelman conducts a global study of trust looking

at levels of trust in 26 countries in government, business, NGOs and the media.[2]   Part of their research involves looking at how much people trust the leaders in these four different spheres of society. To measure this they have created the Edelman Trust Barometer. The Trust Barometer identifies 16 specific attributes which build trust and clusters them into five groups; engagement, integrity, products and services, purpose and operations.   The language they use perhaps needs some interpretation, but looking at these 16 attributes in the light of our businesses, churches and families gives a useful checklist for seeing how well we build trust.

When going through the checklist, a useful question to ask might be; 'how would others score me in these areas'? Try and put yourself in their shoes. If you're really brave, perhaps ask them to score you, but make sure you give them permission to be completely honest and don't get defensive at the results if they are not what you expected!

Score yourself between 1 and 5 for these 16 attributes with 5 being very good and 1 very poor. Do the same exercises for whichever elements apply to you; business, family and church and see if there are differences between the areas.

Edelman Attribute – focused on business	What it might look like in the church	What it might look like in a family
Engagement		
Listens to customer needs and feedback	Listens to the needs of the church and their ideas for improvement	Listens to the family and responds to their needs
Treats employees well	Honours the church members	Creates culture of love, honour and respect
Places customers ahead of profits	Places the health of the church members ahead of increased numbers	Puts family ahead of work or ministry
Communicates frequently and honestly on the state of the business	Communicates frequently and honestly on what is working and isnt working in the church	Is open and honest about key decisions the family makes and reasons for them
Integrity		
Has ethical business practices	Demonstrates high levels of ethics in relation to other churches and ministries	High levels of ethics in terms of finances and relationships
Takes responsible actions to address an issue or crisis	Takes responsible actions to address an issue or crisis	Takes responsible actions to address an issue or crisis
Has transparent and open business practices	Transparent finances and decision making and pastors the church well	Transparent finances and decision making
Products and services		
Offers high quality products and services	All areas of church are done well: worship, community, justice	Family life is enjoyed by all
Is an innovator of new products, services or ideas	Innovates ways of improving areas of church or extending the kingdom beyond the church	Comes up with ways of making family life even better
Purpose		
Works to protect and improve the environment	Works to see justice in the local and wider community	Does something about need beyond the family
Addresses societies needs in everyday business issues	Makes social action part of normal church life	Does something about need beyond the family
Creates programmes that positively impact on the local community	Extends the kingdom into the community	Does something about need in the community
Partners with NGOs, government and 3rd parties to address societal needs	Partners with other churches and ministries to extend the kingdom	Looks beyond the immediate family to help others
Operations		
Has highly regarded and widely admired top leadership	Has highly regarded and widely admired top leadership	Acts as a 'spiritual head of the home'that leads the household to a deeper relationship with God
Ranks on a global list of top companies	Is part of a well-known and respected church group	Has a reputation for being loving and giving
Delivers consistent financial returns to investors	Is always growing particularly through new Christians	Is demonstrating the fruits of the spirit in family life

The table is fairly self-explanatory for business but perhaps some added interpretation could be useful to apply for some of the attributes for the church context. I've used some of my experiences of churches to illustrate how some of these attributes relate to church life and healthy church leadership.

Listens to the needs of the church members and their ideas for improvement – part of the role of leading a church is being a pastor, a shepherd who protects them. Most churches are pretty good at this and are run by pastors (as in the sense of Ephesians 4, not just the title). However this can be eroded by a tight knit leadership team that becomes exclusive so that other's views can't be heard. This must be balanced with the fact that a church leader is primarily tasked with doing God's will not the congregation's will

Treats the congregation well – most churches I have been in are fantastic at thanking the efforts of the entire congregation and supporting them in difficult times. The danger is perhaps putting too much on members of the congregation and not allowing them time to rest and be, rather than do and serve.

Places the health of the congregation ahead of increased numbers – it is possible for a congregation to feel the pressure of the commission to make disciples without feeling fully equipped and supported in their journey of becoming disciples themselves.

Has a highly regarded and widely acclaimed top leadership – at the time of writing I am just back from Focus, the Holy Trinity Brompton (HTB) church holiday for HTB and its associated churches. I don't have a long involvement with HTB but as an observer from the outside looking in, the trust that the people there have for Nicky Gumbel, the leader of HTB was almost astonishing. Now I'm sure there are many reasons for this trust, not in the least because over many years Nicky has proved himself as completely trustworthy. However, it seemed to me that part of the trust was from a healthy sense of pride of having a leader like Nicky, who is acclaimed across the globe as not only the leader of a vibrant and growing church movement, but as the pioneer of the Alpha course that has had more than 24 million people attend worldwide.

Is part of a well-known and respected church group or is a well-known and respected church – congregations are proud to be part of something that is seen as working well and being successful, just like employees of businesses are. I think this is a good thing as long as the criteria for measuring success in a church context are sensible. When HTB partnered with a church in Norwich, it created a sense of excitement and anticipation. When other church groups such as Hillsong or Bethel do something, it creates excitement and anticipation and the people who are part of those churches have a healthy sense of pride for being part of them.

Trust and culture

It is interesting and useful to look a bit deeper into the Edelman report as it shows some cultural trends in trust that identify some of the barriers we might face as we look to build trust.

Levels of trust vary from country to country, ranging from a score of 80 for China, down to 36 for Russia. The scores reveal, not only the way business is done or perceived to be done in these countries, but also the levels of trust in the different cultures. The culture of trust that exists in a country will have an impact on the levels of trust in your organisation. Individuals are impacted by the prevailing culture and as a result, view events, organisations and people through the lens of that culture. Both the US and UK come in the middle of the league table of trust. The US scores 59 and the UK 53 although both of the scores are up considerably from the year before.

What does the bible say about trust?

We have God's delegated authority here on earth, are made in the image of God and are called to draw people close to God. Therefore we are called to also reflect God's personality of being trustworthy and of trusting others; giving freedom rather than controlling them.

As we saw in the parable of the prodigal son, the trustworthiness of the father created the conditions for the son to come home and to be restored into his identity. It is the same for us, the trustworthiness of our father creates the conditions for us to step out in faith and live a life of fullness. If we can model this same characteristic, it releases others to live a full life and become the people they were created to be.

So when and how do we trust God? What is it about him that makes him so trustworthy and how can we develop our character?

The Psalms are full of examples of when and why we need to trust God:

We trust in him because he never forsakes those who seek him (9:10), because of his unfailing love (13:5), because he rescues and delivers us (22:8), because he doesn't let us be put to shame and doesn't let our enemies triumph over us (25:2) and because he brings us joy and blesses us when we trust him (84:12, 86:4).

In other words we trust him because he is good, because our best interests are important to him and he will never let us down.

The story of Abraham and Isaac is a great example of trusting in the goodness of God. Abraham's trust released him into the fullness of the promises that God had made to him.

Abraham had previously been promised he would be the father of nations and that he would have more descendants than can be counted (Gen 17). He was 99 at this point and he and his wife Sarah hadn't been able to have any children. Eventually

Sarah gave birth to Isaac as a very old woman. The promise was miraculously fulfilled, but then God seemingly broke his promise, and therefore his trustworthiness, by telling Abraham to sacrifice Isaac. (Gen22:2) This must have been particularly difficult to understand as God had told Abraham it would be through Isaac that the promise made to him would be fulfilled. Abraham obeyed God, tied Isaac up on an altar, and was about to sacrifice him before God intervened, told him to stop and provided a ram instead. Abraham trusted God so much that he knew God would raise Isaac from the dead if he was to go through with the sacrifice. (Heb11:18) It was because of this trust in God Abraham had, that he was released into the promises God had made to him and that his descendants also received the inheritance that was offered to Abraham.

The angel of the Lord called to Abraham from heaven a second time and said, "I swear by myself, declares the Lord, that because you have done this and have not withheld your son, your only son, I will surely bless you and make your descendants as numerous as the stars in the sky and as the sand on the seashore. Your descendants will take possession of the cities of their enemies, and through your offspring all nations on earth will be blessed because you have obeyed me." (Gen 22:15-18)

Abraham trusted God despite it seeming like there was no logic or wisdom behind what God was asking Abraham to do. Abraham trusted God because he knew God was trustworthy and that there was a greater reality, a greater level of logic that God knew and Abraham didn't.

This has interesting implications for us as we lead our businesses, churches and families. Proverbs tells us to:

Trust in the Lord with all your heart, and do not lean on your own understanding (Prov 3:5)

The wisdom the bible talks about and tells us to ask for is not earthly wisdom based on logic and rationale. It is insight through the Spirit to see the greater reality from heaven's perspective. In fact it is called the spirit of wisdom and revelation (Eph1:17); they are part of the same gift.

The consequence of this is that the decisions we make may not always seem to make sense from a logical standpoint. What God was asking Abraham to do certainly didn't make sense. Abraham trusted God despite this because he knew God to be good. God's character was proved to Abraham through the relationship they had.

The same is true for us. If we are known to be trustworthy then others will trust the decisions that we make, even if they don't make sense and there doesn't seem to be logic in them.

Becoming trustworthy

We can trust God because he is always good. It is this goodness that we need to replicate in our lives if we are also to be trustworthy. Living life by the spirit produces this character in us. It produces the fruits of; love, joy, peace, patience, kindness, goodness, faithfulness, gentleness and self-control. If you met someone whose life clearly demonstrated these qualities would you trust them? Of course you would. It is exactly these qualities that allow you to trust someone.

What is amazing is that pursuing a life that has the fruit of the spirit also frees us into our fullness. The passage from Galatians that mentions the fruit of the spirit is set in the context of Paul writing about freedom.

It was for freedom that Christ has set us free. Stand firm then and do not let yourself again be burdened by the yoke of slavery. (Gal5:1)

As we develop the character of God, through a life in the spirit, we become more trustworthy. As people trust us more they are actually freed into making decisions that help them to grow and live life in all its fullness. Developing this same characteristic actually also gives us freedom and revives our leadership and our life. We are no longer slaves and we release others from also being slaves. This has to be an important part of living life in all its fullness.

Hope

Gallup's research found that 69% of employees who feel enthusiastic about the future are engaged in their jobs compared to 1% who are not enthusiastic about the future. Instilling hope in people is a foundational requirement for leading. Hope allows people to see beyond their current circumstances towards something better.

We need to spend time deliberately creating hope for the future and positioning ourselves to also be hopeful. This can be a challenge and in my experience there are two main barriers to doing this:

- Busyness, reacting to the needs of today
- Difficult and uncertain futures

It is difficult to give hope in situations that seem hopeless. Many of our clients have gone through large restructures and cost cutting exercises recently and, as a result, made many people redundant. It is very hard for a leader to give hope in these circumstances and even harder to do it in a genuine and authentic way that doesn't undermine the trust staff have in them; trust that is very important as we have just read!

Creating and communicating hope for others requires us to be proactive. Hope comes from looking to the future not by responding to the needs of today. Many of us are pretty bad at this and are getting worse. 'Busyness syndrome', as it is being coined, is affecting all walks of life and is actually reducing our productivity let alone our ability to convey hope to others.

Busyness syndrome seems to be created from three sources:

1. Finding self-worth through being busy and letting others know how busy we are
2. Poor skills of prioritisation, focusing our time on low priority tasks that are perhaps urgent but not important rather than important tasks that perhaps don't have the same deadlines
3. A culture of now and of distractions - we expect replies quickly, we get messages immediately on our phones and tablets all of which makes it easier to respond to

small, less urgent tasks.

Busyness syndrome impacts all walks of life; business, church and family. I've observed a fair number of church leaders and leaders of different ministries particularly falling into the trap of finding self-worth through being busy. I don't know the reason why, but I can recognise the symptoms as I have been there myself!

The source of our hope comes from the same place as our trust; knowing that God is good and wants the best for us.

For I know the plans I have for you," declares the Lord, "plans to prosper you and not to harm you, plans to give you hope and a future. Then you will call on me and come and pray to me, and I will listen to you. You will seek me and find me when you seek me with all your heart. I will be found by you," declares the Lord, "and will bring you back from captivity. I will gather you from all the nations and places where I have banished you," declares the Lord, "and will bring you back to the place from which I carried you into exile." (Jer 29:11-14)

When we lack hope it is because we believe a lie either about ourselves or about God and his goodness. It is the same for our churches and organisations. When hope is lacking we need to identify the lie that creates hopelessness.

Have a think about the following areas of your life. Which are the areas that you personally need more hope in?

Area of my life	What aspect of this area of my life needs more hope?
Relationship with God	
Family	
Finances	
Time	
Health	
Church and ministry life	
Work	

Once you have identified where you need more hope, think about why you need more hope in these areas. What are the lies you believe that create hopelessness and what is the truth in the situation?

Area of my life	The lies I have believed	The truth
Relationship with God	*I can never have as close a relationship with God as others I know*	
Family	*Close family members will never get to meet Jesus*	
Finances	*I am always going to struggle to make ends meet*	
Time	*I dont have enough time to get things done that I need to*	
Health	*Family members have suffered from ill health so I will as well*	
Church and ministry life	*I never see the fruit that others seem to*	
Work	*It is always hard and never seems to fulfil me*	

Try and identify areas of hopelessness in your churches, families and organisations. What is the lie behind the hopelessness? The following are examples of lies I hear all of the time in business, churches and families:

- The market is too hard, the clients just don't spend money any more
- The competition can do this better than we will ever be able to
- This change will go badly because they always do and no one likes change
- The new church plant down the road will attract all of our younger members away as they have better music
- We can never have the Holy Spirit show up in power in the way he does at large conferences
- The relationship with our kids / spouse / in laws / neighbours is beyond repair

You get the idea. Identify the hopelessness, then identify the lie that sits behind the hopelessness and focus on the truth, the higher level of truth that may defy human logic, but is in line with our God of hope.

Total assurance

We know that it is right to have hope in all situations, not only because God is good and wants the best for us, but because he has given us total assurance that he will work for the good in all situations. Romans 8 tells us that; *'in all things God works for the good of those who love him'* (Rom8:28). This doesn't say in things where our will aligns with God or in things where we are doing the right thing. Or even; 'when God is in a good mood'. No, this passage says in *all* things. This means we have total assurance that all things that happened in the past, all things that happen in the present and all things that will happen in the future, God will use for our good. This gives us total assurance which is the firm foundation from which we can hope.

The beginning of chapter 8 of Romans tells us there is no condemnation. This means there is nothing we have done that will stop God working for our good and therefore nothing that can prevent us having hope, other than believing a lie that the hope we want isn't completely assured.

Hebrews 11 says that *'faith is the confidence in what we hope for and assurance about what we do not see. This is what the ancients were commended for'.* (Heb 11:1-2)

It was by having confidence and assurance in hope that Abraham, Abel, Enoch and Noah were recorded in history as righteous men and saw the promises God made to them fulfilled in their lives and in the lives of their descendants. It is this same confidence and assurance in hope that will see us fulfil the destiny that God has for us and enable us to release others into a full life.

Our hope needs to come, not from our own understanding and plans, but from knowing our Father. One of my favourite, albeit slightly obscure, Old Testament stories can be found in Ezekiel. Ezekiel prophesied that Nebuchadnezzar would be rewarded for his obedience and effort. However, his reward came in a completely unexpected way. Nebuchadnezzar led a campaign against Tyre and it says that *'every head was rubbed bare and every shoulder made raw'* (Ez 29:18). In warfare at this time, before more sophisticated siege works and strategies were invented, taking a town literally involved men trying to break down the city gates by pushing them down. Their heads were rubbed bare from pressing on the city gates and their shoulders were also sore for the same reasons. I love the strong imagery of this passage!

Nebuchadnezzar's army didn't succeed in taking Tyre. They were obedient to God and they tried with all of their effort, yet they still didn't take Tyre. Does that sound familiar to any of your situations? You think you are doing the right thing and what God has told you, but all that happens is you rub your head bare and make your shoulder sore!

Well our hope comes from knowing that God rewards our efforts and obedience, but not necessarily in the ways we are expecting:

I am going to give Egypt to Nebuchadnezzar king of Babylon, and he will carry off its wealth. He will loot and plunder the land as pay for his army. I have given him Egypt as a reward for his efforts because he and his army did it for me, declare the Sovereign Lord. (Ez 29:19-20)

Because of Nebuchadnezzar's faithfulness and obedience, God didn't just reward him with what he was expecting; he promoted the level of reward! Egypt was a far bigger reward than Tyre and one that was just given without any extra effort needed.

The same is true for us. If we are obedient and our effort is for him, as Nebuchadnezzar's armies effort was, then God is faithful and just and will reward us, just maybe not in the way we were thinking. Obedience cannot be measured by outcome. *God is not unjust; he will not forget your work and the love you have shown him as you have helped his people and continue to help them.* (Heb 6:10)

Compassion

The most productive companies have a leadership culture that focuses on developing and recognising staff, encouraging open feedback and promoting teamwork.

According to research by Christina Boedker, from the Australian School of Business, out of all of the various measurements they looked at in an organisation, the ability of the leader to be compassionate – that is, *"to understand people's motivators, hopes and difficulties and to create the right support mechanism to allow people to be as good as they can be"* – that had the greatest correlation with profitability and productivity.

The field of research that I am involved in, behavioural economics, is demonstrating quite clearly that the old "command and control" style of leadership is not nearly as effective as a "connect and collaborate" style.

Those that lead by intimidation might appear to get results, but they end up being short-term, often causing anxiety in others. This leads to poor workplace morale and staff who either leave the company prematurely, fail to work at their best or become saboteurs. The same is true if you tone down the word 'intimidation' to, leading by the force of their personality. They could be very nice people who are great fun to work with, but a focus on task as opposed to relationship will not get the same results in the long run.

In the past, a compassionate style of leadership was seen as weak and less likely to get results, in businesses, churches and often families as well. However demonstrating compassion, whilst still meeting hard targets and objectives, is actually far more challenging than a more autocratic style of leadership.

But what does compassion mean?

When we talk about compassion, especially in the workplace, it is easy to mistake it for letting people get away with things and not having the difficult conversations that need to be had. This isn't compassion at all. Compassion is about making those difficult decisions and tackling poor performance, but with a focus on wanting the best for the person and helping them to become the best that they can be. This sometimes means compassionately letting people go.

Avoiding difficult conversations and letting people get away with things, is actually the opposite of being compassionate as it isn't helping them be their best and is probably also being unfair on others who have to work harder to make up for the performance of those that aren't pulling their weight.

I designed a change programme a few years ago for a large disabled rights charity. They had a policy that they would actively provide employment opportunities for disabled staff as it was in line with the values of the organisation. However, there was a perception that the disabled staff were allowed to get away with more than the able bodied staff which led to a divide, reduced engagement and ultimately bad relationships and poor performance. The 'compassion' shown to those disabled staff actually back fired as it resulted in a perceived lack of compassion for the able bodied staff.

The following are seven characteristics of compassionate leadership. As you read them try and identify areas that you can work on to become more compassionate.

Listen, listen and listen again- compassionate leaders listen more than they talk. When making tough decisions and facing bad news they don't jump to conclusions but gather more information. They are 'slow to anger and rich in love. (Ps 145:8)

Assume the best in others – a quote I heard recently, although I'm not sure where from, is that when thinking of others we judge their behaviour, when thinking of ourselves we judge our motives. We need to judge others as we judge ourselves and see why they are doing what they are doing and what they are trying to achieve. We also need to see beyond the facts of the situation to the greater truth which is the way Jesus sees them.

Keep your emotions in check – We need self-control so we relate to others as we would plan, not as we would react.

Be interested in others – show that you are genuinely interested in others not just asking questions without really listening. People see through a lack of authenticity so you really do have to be interested in others for them to think you are interested in them!

Accept responsibility - According to Brian Tracy, the motivational guru, the hallmark of a fully mature human being is to be 100% responsible for our lives. Blaming others and creating excuses for our mistakes is one of the primary causes for failure as adults and a contributor to poor mental health.[3] It is only when we accept responsibility that we are able to repent and forgive.

Be open to feedback – feedback shows us the impact of our actions and opens our eyes to things we are not aware off. We must learn to rejoice in feedback, weigh it, accept the useful parts, change things based on useful feedback and not allow feedback to damage us.

Support others in their calling – we must focus on helping each person be the best they can be, whether that is in their career, ministry or something else!

Matthew 9 gives a series of examples of Jesus acting out of compassion. He raised a girl back into life, he healed a woman with a chronic problem that would have made her an outcast in society and he healed a blind and a mute man. Jesus' compassion to restore people back into a full life and ultimately into eternal life, was the driving force behind his ministry.

The Greek word translated as compassion in this passage has the same root as the word guts. Jesus was quite literally gutted at the plight of these people and it was this deep, heartfelt emotion that was part of his driving force in healing them all. Jesus modelled, through his leadership, the need for this deep level of emotion that moves us into action.

How can you increase the levels of compassion in which you lead your business, church or family? If you manage to you will be restoring them back into the promises and purpose God has for their life.

Stability

People want to follow someone who provides a solid foundation; it gives them stability to be with other people who provide stability. I don't think it was by chance Jesus said Peter would be a rock that the church was built on. A rock is stable and to build anything that lasts the test of time there has to be stable and strong foundations. The stability that people are looking for is largely emotional. To provide this others need to know how we will react to situations. I used to work for someone who, when things were going well, was great fun and a joy to work with. When he was stressed, you knew it was time to head for cover as you could see the vein start throbbing on the side of his head and you knew his self-control was reduced. This led to many unhealthy conflict situations and some questionable decision making. The effect across the company was reduced motivation and a work force who didn't really want to be there.

Stability means we are emotionally self-aware, in control of emotional expression, secure, and positive. Many studies have found that emotional intelligence, which includes the characteristics just mentioned, is the biggest determinant as to whether a leader will be successful or not.

What kind of stability do you give those around you? Read the following five statements. Then use a 1-5 (low-high) scale to rate your level of agreement:

___ I have good self-control; I don't get negatively emotional and angry.

___ I perform well under pressure.

___ I'm an optimistic person who sees the positive side of situations.

___ I give people lots of praise and encouragement; I don't put people down and criticise.

___ I view myself as being relaxed and secure, rather than nervous and insecure.

Emotional health in Jesus

To demonstrate stability as a personal characteristic we need to be emotionally mature; something that academia and the business world tells us as well as the bible. However, to really understand what emotional maturity means we cannot separate it from spiritual maturity. The first letter to the Thessalonians tell us that we are made up of spirit, soul and body (I Thess5:23) and Jesus himself said that we must love the Lord our God with all our mind, body, strength and soul.

You can't be spiritually mature without being emotionally mature as it is through our emotions, that many of the lies and accusations attack us and try to rob the total assurance we have. Emotional maturity has many components to it, but I think is deeper than 'emotional intelligence' which is widely spoken about in the business world. It's much deeper and transformative.

Emotional and spiritual maturity isn't about learning new skills to have a better workplace, to preach better or to organise ministry better. It's about being transformed from the inside out. It's about who you are, deep down, and how that impacts on your relationship with God, with others and with yourself.

Peter Scazzero, Founder of New Life Fellowship Church in New York[4] , works with pastors to help them to develop their emotional maturity. In a recent interview Peter said:

"So, for example, at the conferences I do for pastors, we look at family of origin. We do a three-generational genogram and then ask, "How does your past impact who you are in the present?" We also teach things like grieving and loss. How do you deal with loss? How do you process grief? That's an under taught topic. There's a whole book in the Bible called Lamentations; two-thirds of the Psalms are laments. Jesus was called the "Man of Sorrows." Yet, we don't do grieving. We don't do loss. We do bigger, better, faster.

Emotional health also involves acknowledging limits. We don't do limits well in North American culture. But there's a whole teaching on limits in Scripture, about not crossing the line, like Adam and Eve did. We like to think it's our effort and determination that results in great things for God. But in 1 Corinthians 13, we see the most important aspect of maturity is the agape that flows through us, that comes out of our relationship with God. It's the one thing Satan cannot counterfeit".

In his book, The Emotionally Healthy Church[5] Scazzero identifies six principles of emotionally mature disciples. They are:

1. Look beneath the surface – ability to identify feelings, deal with emotions and being honest with self
2. Break the power of the past – understand the impact childhood, past events and previous generations may have on us today
3. Live in brokenness and vulnerability – take responsibility, seek feedback and be honest about weakness and failure
4. Receive the gifts of limits – being able to say no, setting healthy boundaries and creating a healthy work life balance
5. Embrace grieving and loss – openly admit to loss and disappointment, take time to grieve and allow God to work in experiences of depression and sadness
6. Make incarnation your model for loving well – Accepting yourself just the way you are, suffer with those who suffer and rejoice with those who rejoice, rarely judge but

be an active peacemaker. You 'love well'

How emotionally and spiritually mature are you and how does that impact on your stability in business, church and family life? If you can turn stability into a strength, then it will increase the trust others have in you and in doing so, release them into a fuller life. In return it will also revive you!

Reflect on the principles of emotional maturity listed above. Ask Holy Spirit to highlight areas that you can become more mature in. Then ask Holy Spirit to show you what might be holding you back in these areas.

Fathering fullness

Our personal characteristics impact on others. In fact they are a large determinant of the engagement of those in our churches, businesses and families and therefore the fullness of life in which these people are living. Our personal characteristics as leaders are to do with the way we father. A good father is trustworthy and trusting. A good father gives hope. A good father is compassionate and a good father is also stable and emotionally and spiritually mature.

By become better at fathering our churches, businesses and families we release others into the fullness of life and in doing so actually are revived ourselves, living more of the life that we are called to live.

References
1.   Rath T., Conchie, B. (2008) Strength Based Leadership, Gallup Press, New York.
2.   http://www.edelman.com/insights/intellectual-property/2014-edelman-trust-barometer/
3.   http://www.digicast.com.au/blog/bid/91694/Why-removing-Personal-Responsibility-is-Irresponsible
4.   http://www.emotionallyhealthy.org/blog/
5. Scazzero, P. (2010) The Emotionally Health Church, Zondervan, Michigan,

10

Overflowing from our Strengths and Weaknesses

A Gallup study found that when an organisation's leadership fails to focus on individuals' strengths, the odds of an employee being engaged are 1 in 11. But when an organisation's leadership focuses on the strengths of its employees, the odds of them being engaged increase to around 3 in 4.[1] So when we focus on the strengths of those in our businesses, churches and families they are far more likely to be engaged, revived and living the life they were created to live. They are also more likely to overflow and release others into freedom and a full life.

It sounds obvious; we are engaged by doing things we are good at. We only have to look at children to know this is true. Give them something they are interested in and they will do it for hours but if they aren't interested in it they will stick at for only a few minutes, unless they think they might get good at it.

My eldest daughter is a great, but fairly standard example of this. She loves swimming and wants to go swimming as often as possible. However, what she really loves about swimming is backstroke because she is particularly good and fast and wins her races. She is not nearly as good at butterfly and isn't nearly as engaged in these lessons as she is when the lesson is concentrating on getting even better at backstroke.

So it is common sense that we know intuitively; we are motivated and engaged by doing things we are good at. However most big organisations focus on exactly the opposite. They have a competency framework that people are assessed against based on their role and level in the organisation. Where the assessment shows they are weakest the focus of attention rests. It is in this area of weakness that people are trained, supervised and appraised. The result is standard people in standard roles who all complete the job safely and averagely.

Imagine what could happen if exactly the same assessment took place, but instead of finding the areas of weakness, strengths were identified. Development and training was then given in the areas of strength so people became even better in those areas. Roles and responsibilities were moved around so that everyone spent more time doing things they were good at. Each person would come alive and the productivity of the whole organisation would increase dramatically.

In my experience, churches are generally better than business at focusing on strengths, although this is a generalisation. However, in all walks in life there is a strong cultural pressure to focus on weakness rather than strength. We look for the things we aren't good at, often at the expense of celebrating and investing further in the things we are good at and that make us unique, special and come alive.

There was a great example of the value of understanding our strengths at the 2014 US PGA Golf Championship. On the final round Rory McIlroy had lost his overnight one shot lead and was trailing by three shots after the first nine holes. On the par five 10th hole McIlroy drove the green in two shots, the only person in the whole tournament who managed to do so. He then putted for an eagle three catching up the leaders by two shots and creating the momentum that would see him go on and win the championship.

McIlroy's strength is driving straight and long. The rest of his golf game is also very good but it is this strength in driving that makes him unique, different and better than the opposition. It is this strength that is the focus of McIlroy in training. The rest of his game needs practice as weakness leads to failure, but it is our areas of strength that lead to success.

Our culture focuses on weakness due to an unhealthy fear of failure. However it is by focusing on strengths that people will come alive and we will succeed individually and corporately.

The Scientists and Bin Men

A few years ago I was involved in two consulting projects running in parallel. The first was with the street cleaners and bin men of a city in England. The project was to introduce more efficient working processes and improve the effectiveness of the leadership team. The second was with a high tech science organisation. They were the result of the merger of two previous businesses and the work was post-merger to develop a new single culture and efficient and productive working practices. The science undertaken quite literally blew me away and I certainly didn't understand it, but when someone shows you round the site and shows you buildings and equipment with names that sound as if they are out of Star Trek, you can't help but be impressed even if you have no idea what they are talking about!

On the surface the two projects looked very different; bin men in one project and some of the world's leading scientists in the other. However the issues with both projects largely came down to good people promoted into management without necessarily being good managers. In both cases we created improvement projects and identified an internal lead for each of the projects. We then did an exercise to identify and showcase the strengths of the teams. The project leads were then asked to choose people to help them on their projects based on what they now understood about each other's strengths.

I was leading on this part of the work for the project with the bin men and grown men quite literally cried as their peers recognised their strengths and chose them to help on the projects based on their unique strengths. Both projects were hugely successful and showed that focusing on strengths is incredibly powerful whatever your role, academic ability or walk in life.

Uniquely made

A strength is a natural inclination or ability combined with practice, development and hard work to turn it into something we are really good at. This natural inclination or ability is God given.

At the beginning of Jeremiah's ministry as a prophet the Lord spoke to him and said:

Before I formed you in the womb I knew you, before you were born I set you apart (Jer 1:5)

The same is true for all of us. We are all God's handiwork, created in Christ Jesus to do good works, which God has prepared for us in advance (Eph2:10). He has given us our natural talents and inclinations and indeed he has also given us our supernatural talents and anointing. The purpose of all that God has equipped us with and made in us, is to do the good works that he has prepared for us and has called us into since before we were born. The point is they are God given and he has given them to us for a reason! Understanding what our strengths are and investing in them so we get even better at them, could be viewed as nothing more than investing in what God has planted in us so we are ready and able to do what he has called us into.

This should also be the way we look at those in our

congregations, businesses and families. How can we help them to identify and develop their strengths, because in doing so we are helping them to prepare for the work that God has already prepared for them?

Some of our strengths have been with us since we were born, others we discover, and in some cases are given to us, as we grow and mature. Ever since I was young, a strength of mine has been sport. It didn't matter what type of sport, but as long as it involved running and a ball of some shape I have always had a natural talent for it and a passion to get even better. A particular strength I now have, which I didn't even know about until I started work as a consultant, is summarising. It sounds quite a small and niche strength, and it probably is, but I've found I have a natural ability. In one to one or group situations I am really good at taking in all of the disparate views and points and pulling it together into a concise summary of the discussion, conversation or agreement. This started off as a natural ability, as I had never been trained in it, and over time I have got better as I have pushed myself to do this in more challenging situations and with larger groups; all of which has helped me to turn this ability into a strength.

My wife Holly has also developed a strength later in life, but a very different sort of strength, a supernatural strength in deliverance. She has always had a passion for people living in freedom and, through a very specific anointing from the Holy Spirit, has been equipped and released in greater authority to deliver people into freedom. In the same way as a natural strength, she has been created, equipped and anointed by Jesus to do the good works he has prepared for her.

What do you do with yours?

So God has made each of us with unique talents, giftings and strengths. The purpose of them is so we are able to do the good works he has prepared for us and in using them we are engaged, revived and live a fuller life.

How well do you know your strengths and how often do you use them? We need to understand our strengths so we can develop them further and we can use them more often. There are some good tools available to help you identify your strengths but in the absence of them spend some time thinking through the following questions:

What natural talents / giftings / strengths do you have?

How do you currently use these strengths in your work, ministry and family?

What do you do to invest in these strengths and get even better at them?

What else could you do to invest in these strengths?

What could you do to use your strengths more in your work / ministry / family?

What supernatural giftings or anointing's do you have / have been given (e.g. healing, prophecy, deliverance)

How are you developing these areas?

What could you do to develop and grow in them more?

It is really important not to compare your strengths with other people's. We must be like David and praise God because we are fearfully and wonderfully made (Ps 139:14). He has made us a certain way for a certain purpose. Comparing ourselves and our strengths and giftings is not only unhelpful to us but takes our attention off God and onto ourselves.

Leading others in their strengths

Marcus Buckingham suggests the world's greatest leaders believe that with enough development and investment, a person can achieve anything they set their mind to.[1] Instead of helping people to overcome their weaknesses, great leaders find out what a person likes to do and is good at and empowers them to do work they excel at.

In our businesses, churches and families we need to adopt the same approach. We need to help others to understand their strengths; we need to understand their strengths and we need to create opportunities for them to develop into these areas of strength.

In the church setting this means we need to find ways of developing maturity in the congregation. We can't achieve this if we view the members of the congregation as people to help us achieve our vision. The only way we develop maturity is by helping them to find their own vision and empowering them towards that. We need to create leaders not followers.

Liz Wiseman found that great leaders are multipliers.[3] They actually improve the intelligence and capabilities of those around them by two times. Multipliers look beyond their own ability and instead focus their energy on extracting and extending the ability of others. Wiseman found that they don't get a little more by doing this, they get vastly more. She found that leaders, whom she termed diminishers, stifled others and diluted the organisation's intelligence and capabilities. Effectively staff whose leaders were diminishers were working at 50% their capacity.

We become multipliers by focusing on the strengths of those around us and helping them to focus on their God given strengths as well. With a combination of concentrating on their strengths and helping them to understand their calling and vision, we will move our congregations from being consumers to producers. We will engage and enthuse our staff and will revolutionise family dynamics. To do this means we have to accept there will be mistakes and failure and that the achievement of our vision isn't the number one objective anymore. However the way the kingdom works is that when we put others first, we achieve what we need to achieve more easily as well! The last shall be first and the first shall be last.

Look for strength not competence

It is important not to confuse strengths with competence when looking for others' strengths so that you can invest in them. A strength comes from a natural ability or inclination and then needs further development to become a recognisable strength. This means that someone's area of strength may not be immediately recognisable because, in actual fact, they aren't that good at it yet in comparison to others.

So looking for strengths to invest in is not as simple as looking for things people are good at. If that were the case there would be no way anyone would develop into areas they had never tried!

Discernment and insight is needed throughout this process as we need to look at people in the way God looks at them. The story of when the prophet Samuel was sent by God to Jesse's family to anoint one of the sons as the King of Israel illustrates this point perfectly. Samuel went through Jesse's sons looking at their physical appearance and probably their confidence and authority. However God viewed these people in very different way. He said to Samuel:

"Do not consider his appearance or his height, for I have rejected

him. The Lord does not look at the things people look at. People look at the outward appearance, but the Lord looks at the heart". (1 Sam 16:7)

God knew what was inside David and he saw the whole picture. He knew what David would become. He knew the natural abilities and inclinations David had, that might not yet be a strength, but would become so. He also knew how David's character would respond to God developing and promoting him and it was this whole picture that God told Samuel to see.

It is exactly the same for us as we look to raise people up and invest in them. What we need to see is not who they are now, but who they could become. We need this spiritual insight so we invest in the right strengths, as what seems like the obvious strength in someone may not be the area that God is planning on using the future.

The trap of self sufficiency

Having said all of this, there is a danger of focusing on our strengths. The first danger comes if we learn to rely on our strengths and we become dependent on them, not on God. Yes he has given us our strengths to use for a purpose and we come alive when we are using them. However, it is so easy to take that too far that we end up acting in our own strength and not putting our faith in God.

For the foolishness of God is wiser than human wisdom, and the weakness of God is stronger than human strength (1 Cor 1:25).

This passage in 1 Corinthians shows how foolish it is to become self-reliant. My best is nothing compared to the wisdom of God, the creativity of God, the problem solving ability of God...I could go on. Yet it seems to be human nature, my nature anyway, to continually fall back into the idea that; 'I have to solve this problem'.

This is a trap that I have fallen into time and time again

over the last 15 years. When times are bad, there is a problem to solve or something has happened, time and time again I have fallen into a mindset of 'I will sort this out'. This is a very lonely and high pressure place to be and whilst it has always worked out OK in the end, it hasn't been the best way to deal with it! Conversely when things are going well, I praise myself for them and develop new strategies for doing even better. I suppose what I am saying is that I have tendencies to be self-sufficient at both ends of the spectrum, when times are hard and when they are good!

In the last five years this has been particularly evident at work. The economy has been tough for consultancies and we typically don't have an order book further ahead than a couple of months. At times it has been much shorter than that and when a particularly big bill comes in, it really has been hand to mouth at times. I mentioned this to a wise old friend of mine once whose reaction was very different to mine. He straight away said "Hallelujah, what a privilege to have God show you how to have faith in him"! My reaction was very different; I set out to solve the problem on my own, putting pressure on myself and on those around me.

We are made to rely on our Father and be guided by him. Even Jesus said he only went where he saw his father going. If Jesus operated from this position of complete dependence and abandonment then it is so right for us to do that as well. This doesn't mean we throw our brains, thoughts, strengths and anything else out of the window and become 'super spiritual'. It means that our starting place is our Father. Our starting place is to rest in his presence, to hear his perspective on the situation and then to act accordingly. Often he will then use our strengths in the situations we find ourselves in, however he won't always, he will also use our weaknesses so that we learn how to become dependent on him and how to give him the glory.

I once heard someone say that if we blame ourselves when

things go wrong, we will also praise ourselves when things go well. We need to get into the business of casting all of our burdens on him, not relying on our strengths, but relying on our Father.

In recent times I have become better at relying on my Father in situations. The peace I have found in doing this has been immense. It is still a daily battle but it is one that I am overcoming by having a mental checklist that I go through at the beginning and end of every day as well as during the day when I remember. I think of the specific situations I am going to encounter in the day or have encountered and I consciously pass each one over to my father, asking him to be in control and asking for his peace in the situation. When I find there is a particular issue that is stressful and challenging and I can't stop worrying about, I visualise throwing this burden to him. When fishermen cast their nets it is a very physical activity, they don't gently pass them, they hurl them with all their might. That's what we need to do with our burdens; hurl them with all our might to our loving father and say to him 'it's over to you, please take control'.

Theirs is the kingdom of heaven

On the Sermon on the Mount Jesus said; *'Blessed are the poor in spirit, for theirs is the kingdom of heaven'* (Mt 5:3). Wow! I want that. I want my place set up in heaven but I also want the kingdom of heaven to invade my life today and to see it infuse and impact the communities I am part of, the work I do, the friends I have and the church I am in. That makes 'being poor in spirit' fairly important, but what does it mean?

It can seem quite contradictory to other parts of the bible let alone what you have just read about making the most of our strengths! Jesus warns us against having a poverty mindset and urges us to seek spiritual riches instead. *'For where your treasure is there you will also be'* (Mt 6:21). Yet he also tells us that when we are poor in spirit then the kingdom of heaven is ours – seemingly confusing!

Being poor in spirit is the same as being humble in spirit. It is ensuring we do not become proud of what we do or are in Christ; always recognising that it is only by his mercy that we have anything. This sounds easy when written down in isolation like this, but it is actually a great challenge when put in the context of some of the other principles I have written about in this book. We are of royal blood! By that the bible tells us that we are co-heirs with Jesus to the throne of God. We have been given authority and dominion over all spiritual and living creatures on the earth. Through the power of the Holy Spirit we are able to see signs, wonders and miracles and in fact we should expect to. We also know that our personal faith is one of the factors involved in seeing the power of the spirit at work through us. When we consider all of that; humbleness of spirit is actually a much greater challenge.

There is a dichotomy that we need to balance: we need complete faith and confidence in who we are and what we carry as a result of that, but at the same time realise we are nothing without him! If we lean too far down one side of the scales we lose sight of our identity and authority. If we slide too far the other way we lose our humility and are no longer poor in spirit.

Our challenge is to understand our strengths, celebrate them as a gift from God and remain humble in using our strengths because, I for one, definitely want the kingdom of heaven! We must not be self-satisfied or proud in our hearts, sub-consciously falling into the trap of relying on our earthly wisdom, ability and even spiritual track record. If we do, God cannot bless us. The Bible says, "*God opposes the proud but gives grace to the humble*" (Jam 4:6).

Pride can take all kinds of forms, but the worst is spiritual pride. Often the richer we are in things, the poorer we are in our hearts.

What about our weaknesses?

Strengths are so important and are given to us by God through creation. This is particularly true when we lead others, recognising their strengths is vital as it quite literally can bring them to life.

However, understanding our weaknesses is also important as God so often uses our weaknesses to demonstrate his glory. I think it is such a blessing that he does this as it stops us falling into the traps of self-sufficiency and spiritual pride.

In his second letter to the Corinthians Paul wrote:

But he said to me, "My grace is sufficient for you, for my power is made perfect in weakness." Therefore I will boast all the more gladly about my weaknesses, so that Christ's power may rest on me. That is why, for Christ's sake, I delight in weaknesses, in insults, in hardships, in persecutions, in difficulties. For when I am weak, then I am strong. (2 Cor 12:9-10)

In this passage Paul is talking about a 'thorn in his flesh' that obviously was a major hindrance to him and which he pleaded God to take away from him. The passage above is how God responded to Paul. He told him that actually weakness is a good thing because it makes us rely on his grace. It makes us rely on Christ's power to achieve what we have to do and through this reliance we are actually far stronger than we ever could be in our own strength.

If this is also one of the ways God works, through our weaknesses, then we need to know what our weaknesses are so we can spot more effectively how God is trying to use them. In fact a more accurate way of putting it would be to spot when an area of weakness is being called upon and know how to rely on God and his grace and power to achieve what it is we need to.

Gideon the mighty warrior?

One of my favourite stories in the bible is that of Gideon. It is a classic story that all good films are made from; of victory despite seemingly impossible circumstances. The angel of the Lord appears to Gideon and said to him *"The Lord is with you mighty warrior"*. Now at this time Gideon was anything but a mighty warrior. He was the son of a farmer who was in the very act of threshing wheat in the winepress so the enemy couldn't get to it. Gideon was a nobody and a coward. He certainly wasn't the mighty warrior that the angel of the Lord declared he was. Gideon made sure he pointed this out to the angel of the Lord. He began his exchange with the angel by showing just how defeatist he was:

"but if the Lord is with us, why has all this happened to us? Where are all his wonders that our ancestors told us about when they said, 'Did not the Lord bring us up out of Egypt?' But now the Lord has abandoned us and given us into the hand of Midian". (Jud 6:13)

Gideon then went further by making sure the angel of the Lord knew just how insignificant and weak he was. He told the angel that his clan is the weakest of all of the clans and he is the least in his family.

What I find fascinating is the angel of the Lord's reply to Gideon. He said to him *"Go in the strength you have and save Israel out of Midian's hand. Am I not sending you"?*

In saying this, and in his original greeting to Gideon, God was doing two things. He was telling him that he didn't need anything special and he was prophesying life into him. He told him to go in the strength he had. He didn't have any strength, or at least he thought he didn't, but it was all God needed. Later on in the passage the angel tells Gideon that he will be with him and therefore, the impossible becomes possible. Gideon was strong enough because God was with him.

When the angel of the Lord called Gideon a mighty warrior he was also prophesying over Gideon. The act of prophesy calls things into life. Prophecy doesn't predict the future, prophecy creates God's future. As Gideon began to believe the call the angel had put on him and stepped out in faith, Gideon did in fact become a mighty warrior. His strength grew and he led the Israelites to a great victory over the Midianites. As Gideon 'went in the strength he had' (v14) the faith he demonstrated turned his weakness into strength. His feelings of insignificance and despair were replaced with life from God enabling him to do the things he had been called to do and to be the person he had been created to be.

Our areas of weakness are a chance for God to work in us, transform us and for us to co-labour with him to see impossible situations changed. Joel 3:10 says 'Let the weak say I am strong'. It tells us that if we prophesy life into ourselves, God will turn our weakness into strength. There is no situation we face that the Kingdom of heaven doesn't have the answer to and in fact God loves to use our weaknesses so we rely on him and increase our faith in him through that reliance.

So where does this leave our strengths?

So far in this chapter I've painted a fairly confusing picture! I've said that our strengths are God given and we need to know what they are and find ways to use them more. I've also said that we must not become reliant on our strengths and that God loves us to operate from places of weakness so that he gets the glory, we rely on him and our faith grows. So which is right? What do we do?

Both are right, but actually far more important than either is our heart. We need to position our heart so that we rely on God in all things and we are always looking to increase our faith in him and know his goodness more.

In essence we are looking to find the balancing point on the scales where we celebrate the strengths God has given us and look to use them, but also recognise our weakness and our reliance on him.

This is summed up beautifully in Proverbs 30:
Give me neither poverty or riches, but give me only my daily bread. Otherwise I may have too much and disown you and say, 'Who is the Lord?' Or I may become poor and steal, and so dishonour the name of my God (Prov 30:8-9).

When we focus entirely on the riches of the strengths that God has given us, it is so easy to end up doing things in our own strength and becoming proud. On the other hand, when we don't recognise our strength, focus on our weaknesses and spend most of our time in our weaknesses then we end up with poverty of spirit. We become competitive, performance based and jealous of others. Worse than that is we actually dishonour the gifts and the strengths that God has given us and we lose sight of the fact we are sons of God and heirs with Jesus to the throne.

Looking beyond our strengths

We need to learn to live beyond our strengths. Even when we are operating in an area that we are strong in and we know we can do well, we need to learn how to move beyond our strengths towards impossibility. It is only when we move beyond our comfort zone into new territory that we actually hand the reins over to God and say to him, you come and reign. When we step out in faith beyond our strengths and see God come through then we receive a breakthrough that we can steward and move into greater things from. We steward what he has given us and look to multiply it for the kingdom as Jesus taught in the parable of the talents.

References
1. Rath, T. and Conchie, B. 2008 Strength Based Leadership Gallup Press New York.
2. Buckingham, M. (1999) First Break all the rules, Simon and Schuster.
3. Wiseman, L. (2010) Multipliers, How the best leaders make everyone smarter, HarperBusiness.

11

Empowering Others to Overflow and Inherit Overflow

For people to be truly engaged in their work, churches or any other group, they have to be involved in things that impact on them. We see this time and time again on change programmes that we run. If people have been involved in the process and listened to, then they are far more likely to roll their sleeves up and join in with the implementation, even if they don't agree with the decision!

There was one particular change programme we ran for a department of a large NHS Trust, where this was very evident. The Director wanted to change things as he knew there were efficiency savings that could be made, but the department had been very resistant to change and used their experience and expertise in their functional area to convince the Director, whose background wasn't in this area, that there was no way any change would work. Knowing this background we used the people from the department to design the change programme. Our role was to point them in the right direction and facilitate the process, but they did the work. In the end, the department, that had said no change was possible, found £2million savings from a £10million budget and delivered a better service at the end. They were involved and therefore they bought into it and made it far more successful that anyone envisaged.

To be engaged we also need to understand why we are important and significant. Why is our role vital to the bigger picture? If we understand why we are needed and significant, we are again more likely to be engaged. If we are engaged then we are on the road to living in the fullness!

Involvement and empowerment have to be undertaken authentically for them to result in increased motivation and engagement. Many staff in large corporates have a very cynical view of involvement. They are 'consulted' about changes, but in fact everyone already knows that the decision has been made. This form of 'consultation' is common in businesses and churches alike and isn't about the organisation, it is normally about the leader. Their view of leadership is that as the leader, they are the one with the ideas and vision and therefore must ultimately make the decision, or have their way.

This type of involvement can be detrimental to the relationship that exists between the leader and everyone else. However the real impact of it is long term as it creates followers rather than new leaders. It tells people that their role is to serve the vision of someone else rather than have their own vision. It creates volunteers in churches, possibly who give huge amounts of time, but who never walk in the calling on their lives. In businesses and other organisations, it creates people who give the bare minimum and as a result are robbed of living life to the fullest.

Thom Schultz recently wrote an interesting article about the 'Dones'. These are people who are leaving church because they are 'done with it'. This isn't because they have lost their faith, in fact quite the contrary, the 'dones' are typically those who have been very involved, provided lay leadership, financial support and service. They are leaving, as Schultz describes because; *'they are fatigued with the Sunday routine of plop, pray and pay. They want to play. They want to participate. But they feel spurned at every turn.*[1]

We need to move from involvement and consultation to empowerment so we reproduce leaders who will impact the community rather than followers and volunteers who serve our visions.

A definition of empowerment that I quite like is that it is about; "sharing degrees of power with lower level employees to better serve the customer".[2]

Empowerment is certainly about sharing power and not just sharing tasks. Very often we think we are empowering by delegating key tasks to people. However, the fact we are delegating tasks means we are not actually being empowering, we are just asking people to complete tasks that we have already thought about and planned. Instead we need to delegate authority. By delegating authority we are telling people; 'I trust you to do a good job here'. We are actually sharing power, a key aspect of this definition. The definition also has a second part; the power is shared for a reason and that reason is to serve an end goal. In the business context of the definition it is to better serve the customer.

The definition is saying that the best way to serve a customer, which is the ultimate aim of the business, is to empower each staff member to make whatever decision is needed to serve the customer at that particular moment. Have you ever called a customer service department to solve a problem for you and there has been a really obvious solution that you have known and that the person on the other end of the phone has known as well? However, despite you both knowing this, the customer service rep hasn't been able to help you because they hadn't been given the authority to; it 'went against company processes'?

A few years ago I was driving to a client's offices and stopped to fill my car up with diesel. It was early in the morning and I mistakenly filled it up with petrol instead. I didn't realise to begin with and carried on driving for about half a mile until my car cut out on the side of the road. I called the break down service. They got to me really quickly and, whilst they were coming, I worked out what I had done. They towed me to the offices of the client I was working with that day, and arranged for their fuel truck to come and drain my fuel tank whilst I was working, brilliant service! The fuel truck guy did what he had to do; I finished my days work and got back in the car to drive home. All was fine until halfway home my car stopped again. I waited three hours this time for the breakdown service. They got to me and found out that the fuel pump guy had put something back in my car the wrong way round. This meant I had been leaking diesel the whole way and I had broken down because I had run out of fuel.

The breakdown guy was great, gave me the number to call to put in a complaint and suggested that I should get a refund for the cost of the fuel I had lost and possibly the cost of the fuel pump work as it hadn't been done right and had led to a great inconvenience. In total this would have all come to about £300.

I duly followed the process he suggested, put in the complaint and was told to wait for an offer of compensation to be sent to me. I waited a week or so and finally a letter came in the post offering me £15 as a sign of goodwill! I wasn't too pleased and I'm ashamed to say I didn't really feel the goodwill at that point in time! I called the company and ended up speaking to a customer service rep who had no authority to do anything other than to stick to the offer in the letter. It was one of the most frustrating phone calls I have ever had and it probably was for them as well. I clearly explained the inconvenience caused, the cost of the fuel I had lost and the fact it was because their staff hadn't done their job properly that all of this had happened. This last part wasn't quite true as if I had used correct fuel in the first place the whole situation would have been avoided.

The poor customer service rep completely agreed with everything I said, but wasn't empowered to do anything beyond what the letter said. A few days later I spoke to their manager who had more authority and we reached a compromise somewhere between the two values. The manager had the authority to make that decision, which made me happy and meant that their job was actually far more pleasant than the original poor rep. I asked the manager why the original person wasn't able to do what they had done and I got the standard company reply; "they don't have authorisation to do that sort of thing".

If we delegate authority and empower people by actually giving away power, we achieve the end goals far more effectively. The end goals, based on the definition above, are providing the best service for customers. In a church, the end goals must be to worship God with all of our hearts, soul, mind and strength and create disciples who go on and create more disciples. Surely this end goal is more effectively reached if we empower people to do it their way, to find their own vision for what this looks like for them and to then follow that vision. After all, if people are worshipping the way we suggest they aren't doing it with all of their hearts, soul, mind and body because they are following a pattern we set rather than engaging themselves completely with God and worshipping in a unique way and creating their own sound.

Creating an empowering environment

Really empowering people as the norm is rare in my experience. People talk about it and do it in degrees, but really giving power and control away and taking the risk that goes with that is rare. Sometimes the leader at the top may do it, but people further down the organisational structure then become barriers to developing a truly engaging culture as they don't follow in the same path set by the leader. The following are important features of an engaging culture:

Transparent sharing of information – sharing information is important because it not only helps to build trust; it gives employees important information that will allow them to make the best possible decisions in critical situations. Communication, or sharing of information, is often the first hurdle to empowerment as 'information is power'. It is easy to slip into a subconscious mind set of controlling people through the power that is there because we have more information than they do. This is what the Pharisees did in Jesus' time and Jesus specifically warned against the spirit of the Pharisees! (Mt16:6) Often we use information to keep people down without realising it, because we think it is the right thing to do. However, whatever the reason, it doesn't raise people up and empower them. In many organisations I've worked with senior managers who keep much of the unpleasant information about a change programme to themselves, because they think their staff can't handle it. What they don't realise is that the biggest complaint of their staff is not that there will be some unpleasant changes, but that they are being treated like children as it is presumed that they can't cope with bad news.

A few years ago we had a piece of work for a large local authority of one of the major cities in the UK. They had gone through a far reaching change programme and it was going very badly. At the root of the problem was gossip. Wherever you went in the organisation you heard gossip that; 'this is going to happen' or 'that is going to happen', 'they will change this next' or 'they will change that next'. No one knew exactly what was going to happen and in the absence of information, stories were made up that created fear, led to demotivation and resulted in productivity levels dropping massively. I'm sure that if you've worked for a large organisation you can relate to this story. In times of change the lack of information acts as a catalyst for gossip, fear and demotivation. After university I took a year out and worked for Youth for Christ. My boss was a Glaswegian called Iain Bruce who had sayings about everything. One of them was; "when communication breaks down the imagination runs wild". This is so true and is exactly what happened in this case.

The local authority recruited a new interim Chief Executive who I will call Mike Jones for the purpose of this. He quickly realised that stopping the gossip was the single most important thing he had to do. He started to meet with all staff fortnightly, which was pretty much a full time job as there were around 12,000 staff. When he met with them he said to them; *"I'm going to be completely open and honest about everything that is going to happen and everything that is happening. If you ask me a question I will tell you the answer if I know it, even if you might not like the answer. However, in return I want you to do something for me. The next time you hear someone say something about the changes that are happening, say to them, 'did Mike Jones tell you that?' If they can't say yes or you don't believe them, then don't pass that information on."*

Quite soon you heard people regularly saying, "Did Mike Jones tell you that?" and it became a bit of a joke around the place. However it worked! Pretty soon Mike moved the meetings to monthly and then quarterly. Motivation increased and the whole programme got back on track. Why? Because information was used to empower people rather than control them.

Positive risk taking – we need to create a culture that says that it is OK to make mistakes, because it is only by making mistakes that we learn and we do new things. Many of the organisations that I work with are crippled by fear. People won't try anything above and beyond the absolute standard because of fear that they will be blamed and possibly lose their job if it goes wrong. This has such a negative effect on people as the culture that develops stops them from being the people they could be.

Positive risk taking is about managing risk rather than completely avoiding it. A lack of risk taking happens in churches too. In some churches people aren't empowered because they haven't had the right theological training or even that they made a mistake when trying to do something many years before. Now I'm not saying theological training is a bad thing, the very opposite in fact, but it shouldn't be the standard by which the empowerment of people is judged because after all Jesus said that we are all part of the royal priesthood and empowered his disciples who were a complete set of misfits without any training when they were first called.

I think many churches don't take risks because of previous mistakes of raising people up too quickly and too far. It is such an easy mistake to empower people based on their ability or availability when their character isn't operating at the same level. However as I've heard Bill Johnson say, the bigger mistake is often the over reaction from the original mistake.

Celebrate successes and failures – as part of creating a culture of empowerment we need to celebrate our successes and celebrate what we have learned from trying things that didn't work out. The act of trying something new should be encouraged and praised.

The humble leader

To empower people in the ways described, giving away power and control, is difficult and requires a high degree of humility. It requires us to live by the 'last shall be first and the first shall be last' saying rather than just know it in our heads! It means we have to apply what Paul said about Jesus' humility in Philippians 2 to our leadership, whether it is of a church or a business.

"Do nothing out of selfish ambition of vain conceit. Rather, in humility value others above your selves, not looking to your own interests but to the interests of others". (Phil 2:3)

We must value those we lead above ourselves. That means valuing their ideas above ours, their development above ours, their emotional needs etc. In effect it says we must empower them as a priority.

The passage then explains how Jesus made himself a servant to all despite the fact he was the son of God. He didn't use his position or power to get any special privileges, but instead made himself a servant to all. That is how we must lead. We must make ourselves a servant to those we lead, because in serving others we give them power; we empower them.

To do this we need real security in our identity and we must put our faith in God rather than in our own abilities. All areas we have looked at more closely in previous chapters.

Empowerment self-assessment

Have a look at the table below. Reflect on the statements and choose a rating that reflects how frequently it applies to you.

	A lot of the time	Some of the time	Very little / none of the time
I allow others the freedom to develop their own visions and pursue them			
I actively try to raise people who are gifted and talented above and beyond me			
I provide encouragement and make myself available for support			
I help others to learn from their mistakes in a non-critical setting			
I seek feedback from others to find out how I can improve			
I stand back and allow others to take credit for their efforts			
I coach others to help them work out the answers for themselves			
I encourage others to be creative and take appropriate risks			
I actively seek opportunities to develop others			

Inheritance

There is another important area of empowerment that the bible often talks about; that is our inheritance. When we become Christians we inherit so much from God, after all we become his sons and daughters and co heirs to the throne. This means we inherit eternal life, authority, the chance to hear from God and many other things. However, there is also a principle of inheriting from previous generations.

Deuteronomy 29 says *'the secret things belong to our God, but the things revealed belong to our sons for generations'* (Deut 29:29).

This is the way God works. He reveals things to us over time. The bible is the infallible word of God that everything must be judged and weighed by, however God didn't stop talking to his people once the bible was written, he is still alive and delights in revealing secrets to his sons and daughters.

This passage is saying that once there is revelation, once a secret of God has been revealed to man, then that becomes the property of his children for generations. In other words, the children inherit the revelation of their forefathers. The children inherit something they didn't work for, but they can build on.

This principle of inheritance is something that I don't think we do well. Our culture is one of self. We like to achieve things on our own and we have lost the value of honouring and respecting previous generations. Inheritance goes against this culture; we get something we didn't work for and therefore it can't be about self, it is about honouring others.

Church history shows us this is something we have not done well over the years. There have been great Generals of the faith who have had real breakthroughs, God has revealed secrets to them that they have used to great effect, but what they did has not been built on by the next generations. People like the Wesleys, Finney, Roberts and Wigglesworth all achieved great things for God, yet it died out with them and didn't continue. I read recently that if you look at all of the major revivals that have occurred throughout the world in the last two centuries, none of them lasted more than one generation and in fact the average time they lasted was about four years.

To empower future generations requires something of both the older generation who has the revelation to pass on and the younger generation who need to position themselves to receive it.

We will have a look at some of the principles of empowering others through inheritance by looking at some of the famous handovers of power and inheritance in the bible. We will use Joshua's inheritance from Moses, Solomon's inheritance from David, Elisha's inheritance from Elijah and Timothy's inheritance from Paul to draw out some key principles for us to empower others and to be empowered by.

Be strong and courageous

To receive our inheritance we must be strong and courageous. When Moses passed on the responsibility of leading Israel into the promised land he summoned Joshua in front of the whole of Israel and said to him: *"Be strong and courageous, for you must go with these people into the Land that the Lord swore to their ancestors to give them, and you must divide it among them as their inheritance"* (Deut 31:7).

There seems to be two aspects that courage was needed for; firstly to step into the promises of God in the face of opposition from the enemy and secondly courage in dealing with his own people and leading them into their inheritance.

Joshua was to lead Israel into a land that had previously been reported back by the Israelite spies, as full of Giants. They were going into a hostile land with a group of people that didn't have the best track record of bravery. Joshua needed courage to continue to trust God and his promises above natural fear. The same is true for us. We need to learn how to trust God, to increase our levels of faith and courageously enter new territory if we are to receive the inheritance that God has in store for us.

Very often our inheritance, the area we are being called into, is a promotion beyond anything we have done before. We need to be courageous to step into this and continue to build and grow rather than succumb to feelings of inadequacy or awe at our predecessors.

The second area of courage is interesting. Moses publicly warns Joshua to be courageous in the way he splits up the land between the tribes of Israel. Joshua needs to be courageous in the face of the people he will be leading, why? The Israelites, since their exodus from Egypt had been notoriously hard to lead. They had grumbled, complained, worshipped golden idols, declined the opportunity to meet with God personally and instead told Moses to do it for them. There was every chance they would do the same again. They probably didn't have the same level of courage as Joshua and this could lead to fear based thinking and requests of Joshua. Joshua is clearly told that to lead these people, he must focus on what God has promised, not what the people want.

It is so easy for us to lead based on what are people are saying they want and to presume this is good because we are pastoring them, keeping the flock happy, being democratic and affiliative in our leadership. There is nothing inherently wrong with any of these and in fact they can be very positive leadership traits, however they are always secondary to what God is commanding us to do. For Joshua to receive his inheritance he had to be bold and courageous in the face of opposition from his own people. Because he was courageous in his leadership he actually led the Israelites into their inheritance, something they could have missed out on if he succumbed to their wishes.

I have worked with many leaders who have been promoted into a new role. There is an old saying that I have always passed on, that you have a honeymoon period of a month when you first start. During this month you have to be bold and courageous, set your stall out and make changes that need to be made. Being brave and courageous at the beginning leads to greater success later on as you develop the relationship you need with your people and ultimately you also generate respect.

Teachers also have a similar saying. I've heard them say; "don't smile until Christmas". What they mean by that is when they inherit a new class in September they have to set their stall out and ensure they lead the class their way so the class gets used to the right boundaries. Later in the year the teacher can then relax and let more go because they have created the right relationship.

Both examples require boldness and courage as it is easy to be more worried about people liking you than doing things right.

The end of verse eight is very interesting. It says; *do not be afraid, do not be discouraged.* The opposite of courage is not necessarily fear, it is discouragement. Discouragement subtly attacks our hope and expectations and over a prolonged period of time, can be far more damaging than outright fear as it is so much more subtle. Joshua is told to steel himself against discouragement, as allowing discouragement to reduce his expectation or hope will preclude him and the Israelites from their inheritance. Part of being courageous is standing firm in the hope that he has.

When David was preparing to hand the throne of Israel over to Solomon he said to him; *"Be strong, act like a man and observe what the Lord your God requires: walk in obedience to him, and keep his decrees and commands, his laws and regulations, as is written in the Law of Moses. Do this so that you may prosper in all you do and wherever you go and that the Lord may keep his promise to me: "if your descendants watch how they live, and if they walk faithfully before me with all their heart and soul, you will never fail to have a successor on the throne of Israel".* (1 Kg2:2-4)

Again, a key element of this passing over of inheritance, is being strong and courageous. In this case it seems to largely be about being strong in terms of his personal walk and obedience with God. The result of being strong is the fulfilment of the promise to David and the transfer of the inheritance over for many generations to come.

In his second letter to Timothy, Paul reminds him to; *'fan into flame the gift of God that is in you through the laying on of my hands* [his inheritance from Paul] *because God did not give you a spirit of fear, but of power, love and sound mind".* (2 Tim1:7)

Paul is showing here that, not being courageous and succumbing to fear and intimidation will in fact stop the inheritance (the gift from God) manifesting in Timothy's life.

Being strong, brave and courageous is a prerequisite for receiving our inheritance. This takes three forms; we must be courageous in the face of the enemy, we must be courageous in the way we lead our own people and we must be courageous in our personal life and relationship with God.

Know what the inheritance is

Moses and Joshua, David and Solomon, Elijah and Elisha and Paul and Timothy all knew what the inheritance was that they were passing on and receiving. They knew what the promises of God on their lives and for all mankind were, and purposely acted in a way to set the second generation up ready to pass that over. The second generation had been versed in what the promises were and their visions had become aligned.

We must clearly let people know what inheritance we are passing over, or are able to pass over to them. There must be an alignment of vision without limiting the creation of new vision and a hunger to go even further.

Pass the inheritance on further and prepare for it

An important part of the inheritance for Joshua and Solomon was to continue to pass on the inheritance. The point of their inheritance was to create a dynasty, which in the case of Solomon, would result in someone from their family always being on the throne of Israel. Our focus, when we receive an inheritance, should always be on how we continue to pass this inheritance on. Not in the form it was when we received it, but after we have stewarded and increased it. Joshua increased what he got from Moses; he successfully led the Israelites into the Promised Land. Solomon grew what he inherited from David. He created the richest city that has ever existed and one in which no evil was possible (1 Kg 5:4).

David knew that the building of the temple was God's promise and plan for Israel, but he also knew that it wasn't his role to build it, that was for his son Solomon. However David created the environment for Solomon to then step into that destiny. He defeated the enemy, he introduced the non-stop Davidic worship in the tabernacle that created an environment in which no evil could enter the city and he also practically prepared everything needed to make Solomon's transition into his inheritance as easy and as fruitful as possible:

David said, "My son Solomon is young and inexperienced, and the house to be built for the Lord should be of great magnificence and fame and splendour in the sight of all the nations. Therefore I will make preparations for it." So David made extensive preparations before his death. (1 Chron 22:5)

David made extensive preparations to support, enable and further shortcut the work Solomon would have to do. This is also part of empowerment. To empower others we must use our gifts, skills and influence to create the best possible environment for others to flourish in.

David also went much further than just helping with practical preparations; he also extravagantly blessed what

Solomon was to do:

"I have taken great pains to provide for the temple of the Lord a hundred thousand talents of gold, a million talents of silver, quantities of bronze and iron too great to be weighed, and wood and stone. And you may add to them (1 Chron 22:14).

David delved into his riches to bless Solomon's future and calling. He set Solomon on the path needed to build the temple and gave extravagantly towards it. I think the sentence at the end of this verse is also very important – *'you may add to them'*. David gave Solomon permission to go beyond where he had and he also challenged Solomon to do so with this sentence, ensuring Solomon wasn't held back from pushing further for fear of discrediting the name and reputation of his father. When we give an inheritance we must make sure we clearly challenge the other person to take the inheritance on to a new level. We must empower them in deed and word to build on what they are inheriting. All too often moves of God stop as people stand in awe at the mighty people of God and believe they can't add to it. David, the only person in the bible called a person after God's own heart challenged his son to add to it, so we should also.

Hunger for it and serve

Another important principle required to receive inheritance, is hungering for it and honouring and serving those we are positioning ourselves to receive from. In Paul's letter to the Philippians he commends Timothy to them by telling them how faithfully Timothy has served him (Phil 2:22). Because of Timothy's hunger to learn from Paul, he faithfully served him, creating the relationship and the trust in his character that must have been a key reason Paul then laid hands on him, imparting the gift that he encourages Timothy to fan into flames in the second letter he writes to him. Timothy's hunger to learn from Paul and his faithfulness in serving him, creates the environment for him to receive the inheritance from Paul. The same is true for us.

Elisha also hungered for the inheritance that was available to him.

So Elijah went from there and found Elisha son of Shaphat. He was ploughing with twelve yoke of oxen, and he himself was driving the twelfth pair. Elijah went up to him and threw his cloak around him. Elisha then left his oxen and ran after Elijah. "Let me kiss my father and mother goodbye," he said, "and then I will come with you."

"Go back," Elijah replied. "What have I done to you?"

So Elisha left him and went back. He took his yoke of oxen and slaughtered them. He burned the ploughing equipment to cook the meat and gave it to the people, and they ate. Then he set out to follow Elijah and became his servant (1 Kg 19:19-31).

After Elijah had thrown his cloak around Elisha, Elisha immediately left what he was doing and ran after Elijah. He didn't wait for anything, he ran after him straight away. He then went back to sort out his affairs before re-joining Elijah as his servant. However he didn't sort out his affairs as we normally would. He slaughtered his oxen and burned his ploughing equipment. He removed any possibility of returning to his old life. He removed his security in his old life so that he could whole heartedly pursue Elijah and serve him single-mindedly. He hungered after the inheritance that he could receive from Elijah.

Elisha then served faithfully as Elijah's assistant for a number of years before Elijah was taken up to heaven. Just prior to this, we again see the hunger that Elisha had to receive all he could from Elijah. Elisha, Elijah and the company of other prophets all knew prophetically that Elijah was to be taken up to heaven imminently. At three points Elijah told Elisha to 'stay here' while he carried on to somewhere else that the Lord was sending him. This was a prophetic test for Elisha to see how ready he was to receive the inheritance from Elijah.

For a servant to disobey his master, especially someone as

renowned and godly as Elijah, would have been difficult, yet Elisha knew it was a test and knew what was at stake. His hunger overpowered the conventions. By Elijah telling him to 'stay here' three times he was testing to see whether Elisha would rest on the inheritance or whether he would look to steward it and increase it. The same is true for us, the hunger must not just be about gaining what someone else has, but must also be to steward it and grow it further to then pass on again.

If Elisha had stayed where he was those three times it would have told Elijah that he wouldn't have looked for increase, he wouldn't have stewarded the inheritance and therefore wouldn't have been ready or right for it.

In their final exchange together, Elijah asks Elisha; *"Tell me, what can I do for you before I am taken from you?" "Let me inherit a double portion of your spirit" Elisha replied* (2 Kgs 2:9).

Elisha demonstrates his worthiness to receive the inheritance from Elijah by showing that he isn't content to just receive it, he wants more, he wants to steward it so he can do even greater things than Elijah did for the glory of God.

We need the mindset and spirit of Elisha. We must single-mindedly serve and hunger for the inheritance that is available, not just to get it, but so we can increase it for the glory of God.

Elijah is then taken up into heaven in a chariot of fire and immediately Elisha's inheritance is put to the test. Just prior to this Elijah had struck his mantle on the river Jordan, it had parted and they had crossed. As Elijah was taken into heaven the mantle had fallen back to ground. Elisha picked it up and on the far side of the Jordan were the 50 strong company of prophets watching to see what he would do to see if he is a worthy new leader. Elisha picked up the mantle and struck the water as Elijah had done and the water parted. His courage allowed him to step into his inheritance.

This creates an interesting tension with the principle of leading others to find their own vision that is a theme that runs throughout this book. These examples are clearly showing that serving is right and in fact it is because of the period of faithful service that Timothy and Elisha get promoted in the way that they do. So which is right? I think the answer is they both are. The difference in these two stories is that Timothy and Elisha had their own vision and a period of service was clearly a stepping stone on the way to the vision. The motivation of Paul and Elijah was to promote the younger generation, to see greater things than them. Their mindset wasn't to allow them to serve just so their own visions would be fulfilled.

The focus is on creating bigger people. To do that we need to lead people to find their own vision, but often, if not always, that vision requires a period of service to develop character before we are ready for the promotion.

Working across the generations

In all of the examples we've looked at, the generations work together for a period of time. The inheritance doesn't just pass over at death. This is the Jewish culture of inheritance and is important to understand, as the same principle applies to our spiritual inheritance. We don't suddenly pick up the baton from someone who has died or retired, we work with them as part of the inheritance for a season.

There is a wonderful picture of the generations working together in Ezra. This historical context for Ezra is important to the story. Israel, back in the time of Moses, had been told they would inherit the Promised Land and after 40 years in the desert eventually moved into it. However, due to disobedience they got thrown out of it, back into captivity and slavery. They stayed in captivity for many years and eventually King Cyrus allowed the Israelites back into Jerusalem to rebuild the temple.

Ezra is the story of them getting their inheritance back. In one sense it is about getting back to where they should have been in the first place, getting back to the starting line to then push on from there.

When the builders laid the foundation of the temple of the Lord, the priests in their vestments and with trumpets, and the Levites (the sons of Asaph) with cymbals, took their places to praise the Lord, as prescribed by David king of Israel. With praise and thanksgiving they sang to the Lord:

"He is good; his love toward Israel endures forever."

And all the people gave a great shout of praise to the Lord, because the foundation of the house of the Lord was laid. But many of the older priests and Levites and family heads, who had seen the former temple, wept aloud when they saw the foundation of this temple being laid, while many others shouted for joy. No one could distinguish the sound of the shouts of joy from the sound of weeping, because the people made so much noise. And the sound was heard far away (Ezra 3:10-13).

The former temple had been great. It would have been just about the most magnificent building to have ever existed and it had been lost. The older generation wept as they built and praised. They wept at the pain of losing some of their inheritance. They wept at the pain of not being able to pass on the best possible inheritance. They wept because they had seen the former glory of the temple and they were desperate to get it back. They wept as they repented for the part they had played in losing the former temple. However, at the same time the younger generation were shouting and praising the Lord. They had great hope for what was being built. They had great hope that they were creating an inheritance that would be passed on for generations. They were hungry to create something that would last.

Both generations had a hunger to create something magnificent for God that could be passed on through the generations. The pain and anguish combined with joy and hope created a sound of hunger and passion. It created a cacophony of noise that was heard far away and no one could distinguish the hope from the sorrow.

This is inheritance in action. This is the generations coming together and empowering each other. The older generation with wisdom and experience from the past and with a desire and wish to make sure what is built goes beyond their experiences. The younger generation with hope, joy and excitement at what could be and the promises they are stepping into. Together they empower each other. The hope of the younger generation would have rubbed off onto the older generation whilst the experience of the old was invaluable to the young.

We need to empower each other across the generations in this same way. The noise we create must be heard from a long way off as the deep cries of joy and hope, mixed with experience and wisdom, combine to keep on building the kingdom of heaven here on earth.

References

1. Thom Schultz http://holysoup.com/2014/11/12/the-rise-of-the-dones/

2. Kinicki, A. and Kreitner, R. (2008), Organisational Behaviour, Mcgraw Hill

12

Our Authority to Create Cultures of Overflow

Some of you may have read the previous chapters and agreed with the principles. Some of you may have seen how you can create these cultures in your own life and in your family. The problem often comes when we think about creating cultures in wider groups, perhaps where we don't have the authority or influence that we think we need to have the influence described.

It is possible though. Leadership and cultural development doesn't just happen at the top of organisational hierarchies. Many of the most powerful leaders in organisations don't have any formal power, yet they have a large influence on the culture that is created. If you are at the top of the hierarchy, then brilliant, you have a further degree of influence to create cultures of fullness. It all starts with modelling this culture ourselves and understanding the authority that we have, through Jesus, to see this come to pass in our businesses, churches and families. When we are truly living life in the fullness it will always overflow to others. It will naturally impact on the communities that we live in, the workplaces we are part of and the congregations we are a member of. However, for us to live in the fullness and for that to overflow, an understanding of the authority that we have is vital.

Knowing the authority we have in our heads and knowing it deep in our souls are two different things. Having a confidence and assurance of my authority is something I have found central to living a full life and in releasing others into that same freedom. All three of the examples I shared in the chapter three have this as a common thread; I had complete confidence that I was living out the purpose God had for me at that time and that I had the authority to accomplish that calling.

This authority doesn't come from position or recognition from people, but from a deep down assurance that we have God's authority, passed on to us for the assignments that he has given us. Wouldn't it be great if we had this confidence in our authority at all times, not just in our heads but in our hearts and spirits also? This is part of living life to the full. We can change things because that is the commission Jesus has given to us. We can see his kingdom come in whatever walk of life we operate in.

To unpack what this authority is, where it comes from and what it means, I want to begin by looking at John 18. In this chapter we hear about Jesus being arrested, questioned by the Pharisees and then questioned by Herod. We see four different types of authority, three of them are lesser counterfeits of the true authority of Jesus and yet it is these three that we often strive for as leaders or subconsciously settle for. The four types of authority are:

• Charismatic authority
• Religious authority
• Political authority
• God given authority

Charismatic authority

Peter has charismatic authority. Peter is one of those people that others follow due to the force and strength of his personality. He is always the first to comment, to put his view forward and to show his passion. In this passage his passion overflows into an act of violence by cutting off the ear of the high priest's servant. This act showed how much he cared and that he was a man of action. It could have also led to serious trouble for Peter had he not come under the covering of the greater authority of Jesus.

This type of authority is what many of us look for and often think we need to have, or to be like. We fall into the trap of thinking that we need to have a larger than life personality for people to follow us and that if we don't, then we are a second rate leader.

This develops early in life on the school playgrounds where often it is the largest characters who become the informal leaders because they have the most self-confidence at an early age. As we grow up, this mind set often follows us and culture reinforces it.

The church can also subconsciously promote this form of leadership. Leaders in the church are typically those up on stage speaking and many of them are big personalities. There is absolutely nothing wrong with that, but it can be easy for us to hear the subconscious message that we also need to have a personality like that, to be a leader in the church.

I was recently at a conference at Causeway Coast Vineyard in Northern Ireland. Incredible things are happening there under the leadership of Alan Scott. At the time of writing this they have seen around 1500 new Christians in the previous 130 days. One of the things that I loved about the conference was the way Alan led it. He isn't a larger than life, loud leader. In fact he is fairly reserved, down to earth and relaxed. He even ate an apple during one of his talks (it was in context)!

Watching Alan gave me permission to be myself and not feel I have to be charismatic and larger than life.

There is nothing wrong with having a large personality and this can be attractive for others to follow. However we need to recognise that this is a secondary form of authority. Peter failed. Later on in John 18 he went on to deny Jesus three times and at this point was leading no one and had no authority. It was only because of the greater authority of Jesus that he didn't get arrested himself and that he was forgiven and restored afterwards.

If you are naturally a charismatic leader, brilliant, it is a gift from God but make sure you push in for the greater authority as well. If you're not naturally charismatic, then don't try and be someone you that you haven't been created to be, and push in also for the greater authority.

One of the reasons we settle for this lesser authority and we try and become people we aren't, is because this form of personality can often speed up the process of gaining authority. The world teaches us that we need to push ourselves forward; that our gifts must be used and they must be used now. Self-promotion is the mechanism used and selfish ambition and vain conceit are often the motives behind it, even if we hide those well! True authority is God given not handed out by man. Selfish ambition and vain conceit are qualities we are warned about in Philippians 2 and yet they creep in so easily as it is culturally normal.

I struggle in this area. A large part of my job is about winning work, I have to promote myself and my company to do that. I find it very hard not to apply the same principles to my Christian life. However, by pushing myself forward for things I won't necessarily be following the path God has for me. Allowing Him to raise me up and being ready for the opportunities he creates is a much better route. After all, it was God who accredited Jesus to the disciples (Acts 2:22) and it is God who accredited the apostles to the churches (2 Cor12:12).

Let's let God accredit us not our personalities and our self-promotion.

Religious authority

The next area of authority that we see in this John 18 passage is religious authority. Jesus is taken to the Pharisees to be questioned. The Pharisees loved their rules, their laws and their formulas; ultimately they needed control.

They controlled the people by putting in place many laws and rules and used these to suppress, limit freedom and create an environment that they could manage. The laws they put in place weren't just the Mosaic laws of the Old Testament. In fact, in the 400 or so years between the end of the Old Testament and Jesus being born, the number of laws the Pharisees introduced roughly tripled.

The Pharisees gained authority by limiting and controlling people. This naturally gave them authority as they became the judges over people and they were the ones who controlled any freedom that others had.

This form of authority can also be a trap that we fall into. We look to control and limit those that we have authority over, in order to increase our authority. This happens very obviously, but it can also be subtle and creep in because it is so culturally normal. Is your aim as a leader to enthuse others to your vision or is it to bring out the vision and calling that God has put in each person and then to empower them into that destiny? On paper it seems like a small difference, but the reality is it creates an enormous change. The temptation is to focus on creating good followers of our vision because we need a workforce for our vision to be fulfilled and, after all our vision is also God given. However, the vision God has given the people you lead may be different. You have responsibility to help them to discover it, move into it and discover freedom and fullness in it.

Jesus warns against this type of authority specifically in Matthew 16:5. He is with the disciples and he warns them against the yeast of the Pharisees and Sadducees. He describes it as yeast because a small amount of it affects the whole batch of dough. It spreads and can infect and grow without us realising it. He warns against this because the need to control things is so 'natural' and so subtle that it can creep into our leadership without us realising. When it does it means those we lead aren't living in the fullness of life and neither are we.

I love the way John Eldridge describes the religious spirit in his book Beautiful Outlaw. He says that ever since the curtain in the temple was torn in two from top to bottom, the church has been trying to stitch it back up! We are all part of a royal priesthood and therefore we must fight against the conscious and sub conscious urge to increase our authority by increasing our control and reducing others' freedom by creating laws and rules that control, reduce freedom and limit the belief that we can all enter the holy of holies and be part of the royal priesthood

Political authority

The next form of authority we see in John 18 is the political authority that Herod has. This authority comes from keeping people happy, building alliances and compromising. We see in this passage that Herod didn't want to kill Jesus; he saw no reason to and thought it was wrong. However because of the form of authority he had, he let an innocent man die a brutal death.

This form of authority is also something that the world and the culture in which we live, says is not only okay, but is something that we should get better at. We should build alliances with people in power and people who agree with us to strengthen our position and gain credibility for what we are saying or promoting. In the Christian world we should get to know big name speakers and Christian celebrities to increase our credibility. Or perhaps we should round up other like minded people in our church so we can petition the church leader to change.

Keeping people happy and compromising are not wrong in themselves, but it is the context that makes them wrong. When we make people happy and compromise at the expense of doing what we know to be right, then we are wrong.

In his book 'Culture of Honor', Danny Silk gives great examples of pastors who have led their churches worrying more about what the people want than what God is saying. This is political authority. The same can happen in the workplace, we worry more about what people want, both our staff and other stakeholders, resulting in us compromising beyond what is right.

I'm certainly not saying that we should become autocrats or dictators. Part of being a good leader is recognising that we don't have all the answers and that those we lead are talented and gifted. What I am saying is that doing the right thing is more important than keeping people happy and gaining authority through alliances with others.

Political authority is also the root of gossip. Gossip is driven by the need to build alliances either for or against a certain person or position. Gossip discredits those who don't think like us and creates bonds with those who do in order to strengthen our position and ultimately gain authority over the situation. I'm sure you all have experienced gossip at work, church or between parents on the school playground. It always tries to create power by discrediting opinions and people.

The Sadducees had the same form of political authority. They had to keep Rome happy and side with them on matters that were important to the empire. However in the Sanhedrin, they also had to side with the Pharisees because the Pharisees had the support of the people. The life of a Sadducee was one of political compromise between Rome and the people and through this compromise they found their authority.

In Matthew 16 Jesus also warns about the yeast of the Sadducees. Looking for political authority creeps up on us, is subtle and is justified by society. However it is authority from man and again usually comes from selfish ambition, vain conceit and self-promotion. Let's let God promote us.

God given authority

In John 18 we also see real authority, the God given authority that Jesus demonstrates through the events described. There are three characteristics of this authority that jump out from the page:
- It is powerful
- It is a higher form of authority
- It focuses on purpose not self

Powerful authority

Early in this chapter, as the guards come to arrest Jesus, we see that the guards all fell over when Jesus told them who he was.

Jesus, knowing all that was going to happen to him, went out and asked them, "Who is it you want?" "Jesus of Nazareth," they replied. "I am he," Jesus said. (And Judas the traitor was standing there with them.) ⁶ When Jesus said, "I am he," they drew back and fell to the ground (Jn 18:4-6).

Wow! This is one of the many verses in the bible that it is easy to overlook but when you really do stop and take notice, it blows your mind.

Imagine the situation in modern day times. The Police come to arrest someone. They ask them who they are in order to check they are arresting the right person. When they tell them their name, the power and authority that comes with that name, literally makes the Police stagger backwards and fall over. It is almost unimaginable, yet that is exactly what happened here. The authority that comes from the name of Jesus is so great that the guards sent to arrest him can't stay on their feet. With authority like that Jesus could have done what he wanted, but he knew the higher purpose at stake so he carried on with the plan.

A higher form of authority

The authority that Jesus has runs rings around the other forms of authority that are evident in this passage. Twice in this chapter we see verses that say, 'this happened so that Jesus would fulfil the prophecy'.

Jesus answered, "I told you that I am he. If you are looking for me, then let these men go." This happened so that the words he had spoken would be fulfilled: "I have not lost one of those you gave me." (Jn 18: 8-9)

Pilate said, "Take him yourselves and judge him by your own law."

"But we have no right to execute anyone," they objected. This took place to fulfil what Jesus had said about the kind of death he was going to die. (Jn 18: 31-32)

In both of these events the authority Jesus had was so great that he made the events turn out a certain way so that prophecies would be fulfilled. He had absolute control over the situation because he had so much authority.

Focuses on purpose not self

Through the power that Jesus possessed he could easily have gotten himself out of this situation. In fact just through implementing some of the other forms of authority, particularly political authority, he could probably have talked himself out of being crucified. But Jesus knew God's higher purpose. He knew what he was called to and this was central to his authority.

Implementing this model of authority that Jesus gave us is easier to grasp in a church setting and perhaps trickier in the workplace. The other forms of authority are not necessarily wrong in the workplace as long as the motives and intent are good. However, I am convinced that they are still secondary in power and effect to utilising the God given authority we have in the workplace. We must make sure that the higher purpose that comes with God given authority is always at the front of our minds and always the focus of what we are trying to achieve.

There are some great examples of famous biblical figures that relied only on God given authority rather than the other forms. It turned out pretty well for Joseph, Daniel and Eliakim! To rely on God given authority and not the authority we create, we have to be confident that we have it – so let's look at how we know we have this God given authority and what it give us authority over.

The keys of authority

In the letter to the church in Philadelphia, in Revelation, John begins by writing; *'these are the words of him who is holy and true, who holds the key of David. What he opens no one can shut and what he shuts no one can open'* (Rev 3:7). John is describing Jesus and is writing about the authority that Jesus has. This passage has strong links to Isaiah 22:22 which also mentions the keys of David:

I will place on his shoulder the key to the house of David, what he shuts no one will open and what he opens no one will shut (Is 22:22).

This passage is talking about someone called Eliakim who is replacing Shebna as the steward of King Hezikiah's household, but it is also a prophetic statement about Jesus coming and the authority that he will have. These two passages give some really interesting insight into Jesus' authority.

In the Isaiah passage Eliakim is given a robe, a sash or belt and a key on his shoulder (Is 22:20-25). Each of these has prophetic significance for the authority that Jesus has:

The robe – the robe represents credibility and that the authority rests in the rightful place. There is also a clear link here to spiritual authority as the robe or mantle is a symbol used elsewhere in the bible to represents spiritual authority and anointing.

The sash or belt – the belt represents permanence and action. One translation puts verse 21 as 'bind your girdle upon him'. This shows that once given authority by God we are bound to him. The root of the word for belt comes from the phrase to 'gird up' typically for work or war, suggesting that action results from this authority.

The keys – the keys are a visual representation of authority so that others know who has authority, they are on the shoulder so they are ready for use at all times and they also serve as a reminder of the responsibility that comes with authority. The keys in this time would typically have been very large and heavy so having them on the shoulder would literally have weighed heavy.

It is useful to also look in more detail at what the keys represent. The keys for a royal household, such as the one over which Eliakim was steward, would have probably been for four main areas of the household: the gates, the doors, the armoury and the treasury and these also have prophetic significance.

The gates – a gate is a place of transition; from inside the city to outside, from in the garden to the street. Here the gate signifies the transition from the spiritual realm to the earthly realm, from heaven to earth. Jacob, after his dream at Bethel in which there was a ladder up to heaven with angels ascending and descending said: *"How awesome is this place! This is none other than the house of God; this is the gate of heaven"* (Gen 28:17). The key to the gate gives authority over this transition.

The doors – a door is the way to enter and leave a room. In John 10:9 Jesus says; *"I am the Door; anyone who enters in through Me will be saved (will live). He will come in and he will go out [freely], and will find pasture."* It is through the door that we are not only saved but we also come into the presence of God.

However, as this verse shows it is a continual process of coming in and going out. We come into His presence only to also leave again taking His presence with us. The moment we leave the invitation is there to come back into His presence, to be refreshed ready to carry it out again to extend the kingdom.

The armoury - the armoury is used to defend the house against attack, but also to extend the influence of the house by going on the offensive. This was the authority Jesus had, to extend the kingdom of God.

The treasury - in the treasury is everything of value. This includes our giftings, anointing and calling.

So this is a picture of what Jesus has authority over; the transition between heaven and earth, our relationship with God, extending the kingdom and our gifts, anointing and calling. But what is the purpose of the authority? The passage shows us three main purposes behind the authority: to steward, to father and to glorify God.

To steward - The position that Eliakim is given is described as a steward of the household (Is 22:15). A steward wasn't just tasked with maintaining the status quo, but was also in charge of developing the household and increasing the prosperity of it. Jesus also taught about stewarding through many of his parables, notably the parable of the mustard seed and the parable of the talents. The mustard seed starts small and grows into a mighty tree. The servants who delivered a return on investment for the master were the ones who were praised and rewarded.

To father - Eliakim is described as the father to those who live in Jerusalem and Judah (Is 22:21). This means he had a role of nurturing, protecting, developing and building the rest of the household but also these wider geographical territories.

To glorify God - the passage says that Eliakim will become a seat of honour for his father. In other versions 'seat of honour' is translated as the 'throne of glory' and 'father' is translated as 'house of God'. Whichever translation is right;

this gives the dual purpose of glorifying God and his church by actually becoming a throne or a seat on which God can sit, through the authority that he has given us.

So this is a picture of the authority Jesus has and this is also the authority that he has passed onto us and that he delegates to us as we rule over the earth on his behalf.

In Matthew 16:19 Jesus says to Peter *'I will give you the keys to the kingdom of heaven: whatever you bind on earth will be bound in heaven; and whatever you loose on earth will be loosed in heaven'*. Jesus is passing this same authority that he has, over to Peter and to all believers!

We have authority over the gates, the doors, the treasury and the armoury. We have been given the robe, the belt and the keys. We are tasked with stewarding, fathering and glorifying God with this authority.

Jesus is specifically showing that the authority he is passing onto us is spiritual by changing the *'the door he shuts'* in Isaiah 22 to *'what will be loosed on earth will be loosed in heaven what is bound on earth will be bound in heaven'* in Matthew.

Where does this authority come from?

The authority comes from knowing who Jesus is and having an intimate friendship with him. The verses preceding this passage in Matthew 16 are when Jesus asks the disciples if they know who he is. Peter replies that he is the Christ. Peter understands the identity of Jesus, not just in knowledge but in heart. Later on in the chapter we see a demonstration of the deep friendship Peter and Jesus have: Once Jesus passes the authority over to Peter he then starts to share heaven's secrets (Mt 16:21), specifically in this case, the plans for the crucifixion. Peter tries to talk Jesus out of it and Jesus responds with the incredibly harsh words, *'get behind me Satan'* (Mt 16:23). I believe this actually shows us the deep friendship and love that these two men had and that was central to Peter knowing who

Jesus was. Satan often tempts us in our area of greatest weakness and I reckon at this point Jesus' greatest weakness was his friendship with Peter. The thought of terminating that friendship prematurely was what tempted Jesus most, not actually going to the cross. Maybe Jesus said to Peter; 'get behind me Satan', because the friendship with Peter was actually an area of weakness for Jesus because he felt so deeply for him.

So our authority comes from our friendship with Jesus, understanding in our hearts who he is and our identity and authority that we find through our union with Him.

The authority also comes from hearing God. When Peter says that *'you are the Christ'*, Jesus said to him; *'you know this because it was revealed to you by my Father'* (Mt 16:17). Peter's authority comes from hearing God, understanding his will, his heart and hearing his secrets. In a simple way this defines the prophetic; a gift that we are told to eagerly desire and which is available to us all.

This authority is given by Jesus, not man, but is recognised by man. In Matthew, Jesus gives Peter the keys to the kingdom of heaven and in Isaiah it is clearly God who instigates giving the key to Eliakim. However the symbolism of the keys suggests strongly that this authority is also obvious to man. In fact in the case of Eliakim, King Hezikiah would have to have been actively involved in passing the authority over to Eliakim.

The passage in Revelation also gives further pointers as to where the authority comes from. It says it comes from: *'keeping my word'* (Rev 3:8), *'enduring patiently'* (Rev 3:10) and *'holding on to what you have'*. (Rev 3:11)

This is the authority that we can have. Walking in this authority enables us to live a revived and full life and to lead others also into a life of fullness.

Understanding our authority provides the foundation to change ourselves and develop cultures of fullness that will change those we are leading and overflow into our communities. As you implement some of the ideas in this book keep in mind the authority that you have through your friendship with Jesus. You have authority over the gates, the doors, the treasury and the armoury. This gives you all the authority you need to change the cultures of your workplaces, churches and families and to lead others into a full life and see that overflow.

13

So what next?

Living life in all of its fullness and overflowing into our communities should be our natural state. Jesus came to bring life in all of its fullness, he accomplished his mission therefore it is possible to live life this way. The result of this is we overflow and also bring life to others around us.

We are also called to be like Jesus and release this life in all walks of our life; in church, in our workplaces, our families and our communities. Jesus made no separation between these areas of life and neither should we. The kingdom of heaven is at hand in all of them and it is our task to be transformed so that we can transform. To come to life so we can bring life. When we live life the way Jesus intended; in fullness and with purpose, the only outcome is it also impacts on others around us.

We have a choice to make. Do we want a life like this? It perhaps sounds like a silly question. Who wouldn't? Who wouldn't want to live the life that Jesus intended, especially as it is the best sort of life? One where we are fulfilled and peace, hope and joy are normal. However, we do have to make this choice because we have to contend for this life, it doesn't just happen. We have to align our human nature with the kingdom of heaven rather than have it conflict and draw us back into a mundane and average existence. We need to consciously partner with the Holy Spirit to align ourselves with God and become the people we were created to be and to do the things we were created to do.

When Jesus commissioned the disciples he also commissioned us. What came with this commission was authority, the authority to overcome our human nature as well as the spiritual powers and principalities that battle to stop us living as Jesus intended. We have the authority to overflow and to lead others into overflow.

To do this we need a vision and we need purpose. We need to dream with God to find out the plans and purposes he has for us. We also need to lead other people in a way that they find their vision and purpose, which might not be serving our vision.

We need to live purposefully and overcome our habits. In fact we need to go beyond that and create new habits of resting in God's presence. To do this we must brace ourselves to the Word and contend to be the people we were created to be, whilst at the same time, inviting the Holy Spirit to renew us.

We need to be aware of the influences that impact on our thinking, our emotions and our actions. We need to replace negative influences with the influence of the presence of God and when we can't remove ourselves from unhealthy culture; we need to learn how to rise above it as Daniel did.

We need to cultivate healthy expectations of what God can do through us as the level of our expectation creates the depth of the invite for God to come and use us. To do this we need to understand our identity as sons and daughters of God and the authority that comes with this. Not just understand in our heads, but know it in our hearts.

We battle against fear and loss to maintain our expectations. By knowing more of God's goodness we are able to overcome these emotions and maintain our deep assurance of who we are and what we are capable of because Christ is in us.

Good fathers create the environment for their children to grow and flourish. We need to develop the characteristics of good fathers to release others into the fullness of life and, in so doing, also further overflow ourselves. We need to make trust, hope, compassion and stability characteristics that we are known by.

Understanding and using our strengths develops the God given gifts that are in us. We have to learn how to use them, but without relying on them. We need to move beyond our strengths to the impossible so we rely on God in all things and develop our faith in him.

Empowering others to become the people they were created to be is part of discipleship, part of our commission. We need to learn how to really empower people by giving away our power. We also need to learn how to give and receive inheritance so what we learn and grow into can be built on by future generations.

This is our challenge. If we partner with God on this challenge and align our God given human nature with the kingdom of heaven, then we live life as it was meant; full of peace, hope and joy. When we also lead others in a way so they are filled and together we begin to overflow, the impact on our families, churches, workplace and society in general will be immense. This is a culture of overflow.

Do you want to see a culture of overflow in your workplace?

Engaging Leadership Cultures is written to help Christian leaders implement kingdom culture in the workplace. It follows the same structure as *Creating a Culture of Overflow*, but without the biblical references. It is ideal to give to non-Christian management teams so together you can create a culture that releases your staff into greatness and in so doing increases productivity and results.

It has been used successfully in local authorities, NHS Trusts, large private sector corporations, smaller businesses and charities.

Available on Amazon or for orders of 8 or more please contact support@engage-deep.co.uk

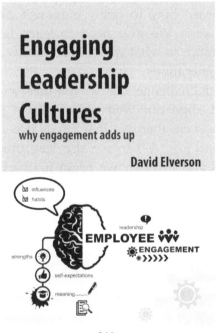

About the Authors

David Elverson is a management consultant living in Norwich, England. He specialises in culture change and works with big business, the public sector and church groups to develop new cultures that bring life to the organisations. David's passion is to see the church prepared as the beautiful bride ready for the wedding. He and his wife lead Global Legacy in the East of England; supporting church leaders and leaders in the market place to see revival come in their contexts.

David is married to Holly and has two young girls.

For business or church speaking or consulting enquiries please contact david.elverson@engage-deep.co.uk

Paul Manwaring is a pastor and a member of the senior management team at Bethel Church in Redding, California. His primary responsibilities are to oversee Global Legacy, an apostolic, relational network or revival leaders, and to equip and deploy revivalists through his oversight of the third-year programme in Bethel's School of Supernatural Ministry (BSSM).

Paul truly carries the gift of administration/government and releases that power and wisdom through his Supernatural Strategic Planning Workshops, his itinerant ministry, and his teaching at BSSM. His passion is to see the Bride prepared, glorious sons and daughters revealed, cancer destroyed, and cities transformed as the government of heaven is established on earth.

Paul came to Bethel in 2001, after leaving a career in senior prison management in England. He holds a master's degree in management from Cambridge University and is a registered general and psychiatric nurse.

Visit Paul's website at: www.paulmanwaring.com

Lightning Source UK Ltd.
Milton Keynes UK
UKOW06f1440121015